HELL'S HEAVEN
IS BETWEEN MY EARS

(OR HEAVEN'S HELL IS BETWEEN MY EARS)

A POETIC ODYSSEY

ELLIOTT STEIN

Order this book online at www.trafford.com
or email orders@trafford.com

Most Trafford titles are also available at major online book retailers.

Print information available on the last page.

ISBN: 978-1-4907-5030-9 (sc)
ISBN: 978-1-4907-5032-3 (hc)
ISBN: 978-1-4907-5031-6 (e)

Library of Congress Control Number: 2014919441

Trafford rev.   06/01/2015

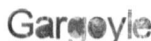

Gargoyle

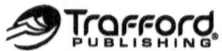 www.trafford.com

North America & international
toll-free: 1 888 232 4444 (USA & Canada)
fax: 812 355 4082

Gargoyle Publishing
A division of:
Gargoyle Productions
United Kingdom
www.GargoyleProductions.co.uk

To Landmark:

The magnificent Communication Course Leaders, Forum Leaders, staff and wonderful graduates.

Thank you for the last 30 years. They were great. You were great.

"I know I am deathless. No
doubt I have died myself
ten thousand times before.
I laugh at what you call
dissolution, and I know
the amplitude of time."
                    – Walt Whitman

"Eternity is a very long
time, especially towards the
end."
                    Woody Allen

Introduction

"Life's a bitch –
and then you write a poem about it"

It's the bitter cold winter of 1986, I'm a twenty-five year old American living in a dingy room in a grimy house share in Woodgreen, North London. It was a depressing house with miserable view from my window.

Directly across the high street was a Greek butcher with a grotesque, disembodied, pig's head hanging from a hook in the window. When I looked out my window I was face to snout with that obscene bacon monstrosity.

Something woke me up. I sat up in bed, wide awake, with a heightened awareness of the reality around me. The surrounding bedroom was bathed in the sickly yellow streetlamp from outside, a woman I was briefly dating was asleep next to me.

I was in the midst of experiencing a life changing phenomenon.

It was a vision, as if a giant, ghostly, wide-screen movie was floating before and around me. I wasn't just a spectator, somehow I was connected to it on an esoteric level that I had never before experienced.

My vision was of a rather dashing man dressed in a WW2 RAF uniform, hat, and sporting a classic 1940's mustache. There was an intuitive knowing, "That's me... and I'm going to die soon."

This former incarnation of myself was sitting in a shadowy pub nursing a pint. I heard a voice speak from inside the vision, "Come on kid – it's time to go."

Time stood still, I do not know how much 'real time' passed while experiencing this. It ended and I was back in the bedroom.

Over the decades, with the aid of some extraordinary psychics, hypnotic regression sessions and research, I discovered a few more details of that lifetime, including my name: David W. Stannard.

The incident helped put life into perspective... not just my life but life itself. My present existence made more sense.

I understood why, ever since I was about four years old, there was such a burning desire to leave New York to live, work and die in London and why I feel so at home in this great city.

It also explained my fear of flying. I ended that last life time as David as a passenger on a crashed military plane downed in Kerry, Ireland, on 28 July, 1943 (which is coincidentally the birthdays of both my father and sister).

Last year, on a ski trip, I met a wonderful woman named Caroline Coxton, who works for the British War Graves commission. She went through the records and actually sent me a photo of David W. Stannard.

The face was chillingly familiar. Through the different skin and bones, I could clearly see myself in the way he looked at the camera.

I recognized the attitude. There was an expression he had that was exactly like my often feigned, pained, sarcastic look. It conveyed, "Do I really have to stand here, try to look dignified, and have this ridiculous photo taken?"

*   *   *

When we are born, we still retain the memories of all the lives we lived as well as the afterlife. This 'remembering' slowly fades as we become more and more immersed and trapped in this construct that we call reality or life.

This is the story, told in poetry and connecting narrative, of an old soul beginning its current incarnation. It's the experience of an infinite consciousness struggling to hang on to the memories and many identities of countless lifetimes. This consciousness pieces the different events of his/her former lives and tries to hang onto who he or she really is before forgetting and playing the latest game of life.

*   *   *

Thank you for buying or downloading or borrowing or stealing this book.

And – thank you for loving it, hating it or just being indifferent.

If I am alive and FEELING something, anything... it's time to write a poem. Poetry, in short, is my salvation. It keeps me sane, although many who know me will argue that it hasn't been doing a good job of that.

As a writer, poetry is the closest I can get to pure artistic expression.

I usually write for film, TV, radio, the stage and books. I have to be mindful because if I write something too edgy, uncommercial or offensive then the project won't get funded, script won't be picked up, book won't get published... and I won't get paid.

More often than not, film scripts that I've developed for years never get commissioned or green lighted. Most of my best work will never see any light of day beyond the hard drive of my computer for a variety of reasons (including the reason of it sucking).

I discovered that the world won't end in ice or fire... it will end in a sanitised fart of political correctness. My hard drive is littered with aborted projects that flowed down the pipeline until it just happened to offend the wrong politically correct person. It is just too easy to offend people, all I have to do is wake up in the morning.

Then there are the projects that make it which, along the way, have been edited by careful committees and become ball-less, soul-less, white bread blandness.

My poetry is different – it is pure (and if you think my poetry is crap… at least it is pure crap). I write it free from commercial considerations. When writing, there is just being in the moment and the love of 'the word': creating, playing, noodling and experimenting.

I do not give a damn if that poem ever sees the light of day, if it is successful or if I make any money from it. I don't care if someone finds if insulting or deems it to be crap and decides not to publish it. If it offends you or if you hate it then it is your problem and not mine.

Poetry is freedom.

*   *   *

HELL'S HEAVEN IS BETWEEN MY EARS features poems that I've written over the last thirty-five years, connected by a narrative, and illustrated by photographs that I've taken around the world specifically for this collection (including at such locations as my home city of London, Venice, Tokyo, Osaka, Kyoto, Mexico City, Bangkok, Singapore, Hong Kong, Shanghai, New York, San Francisco, and Seattle).

HELL'S HEAVEN is an experiment in narrative form using the medium of poetry to tell a story in a way which only poetry can express. While the poems individually stand alone, as in a traditional collection, they combine to take you on a 'poetic odyssey'.

*   *   *

Elliott Stein

A journey begins for the man who is not our brave hero.

Since we have no villains, there can't be heroes in this story.

Since nothing has ever ended, and since there is no real beginning, this is as good a place as any to begin.

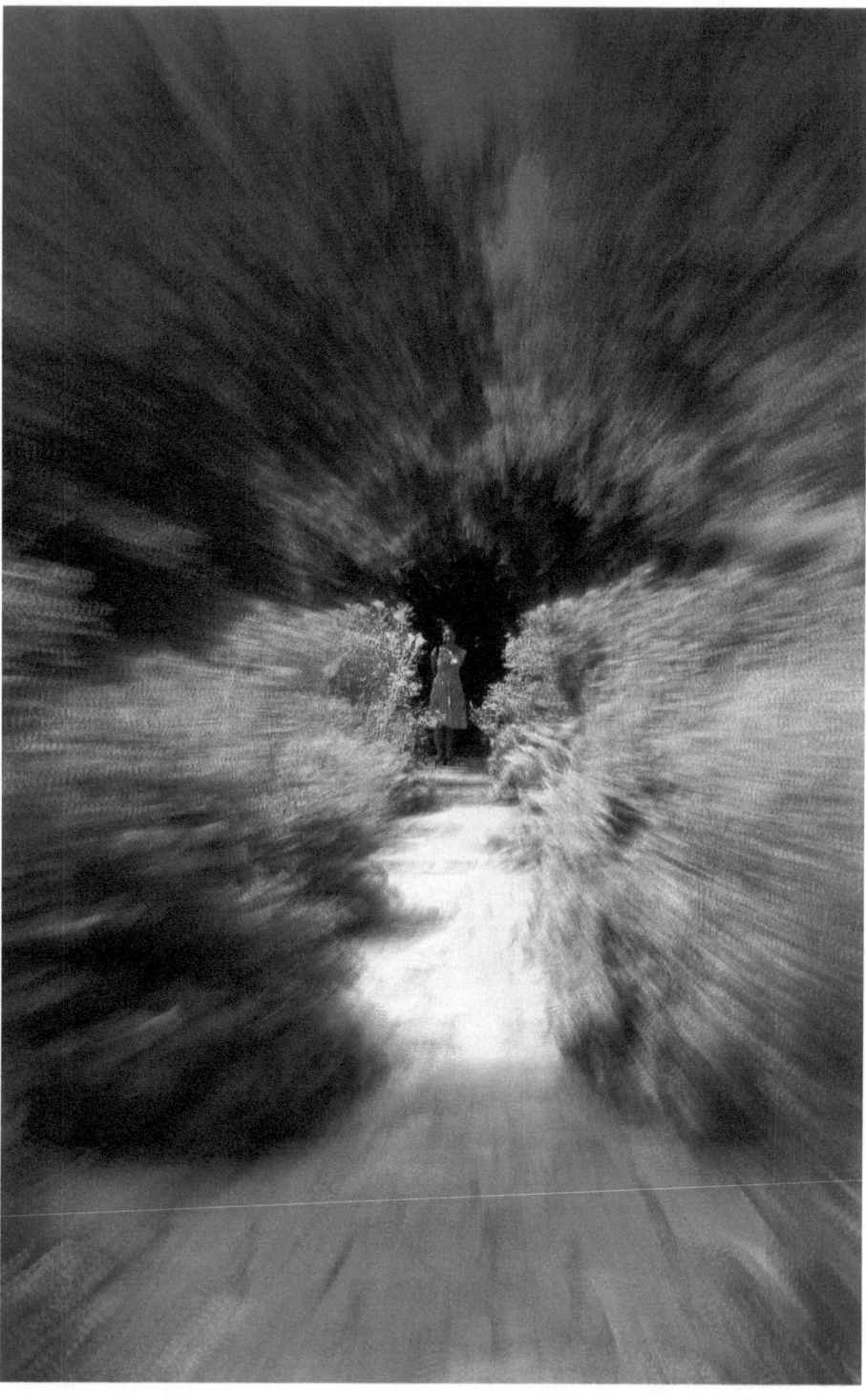

Never Will Always

Tomorrow,
You've just arrived,
Though you've been here from the beginning.

And when you leave,
You never will.
You'll be here,
Always.

After I'm gone,
Though I'll never leave you,
Yesterday.

The Oblivion only illuminates the stark void outside my pram.

If I could talk I would speak, Id reminisce of who I was before.

My head is still a space once filled by true but unfulfilled loves of yesterday.

Elliott Stein

My past is in a sad
blinkered future.

I dwell in the might-have
beens, ponder the could-haves
and never-weres.

I wander, I wax,
nostalgically.

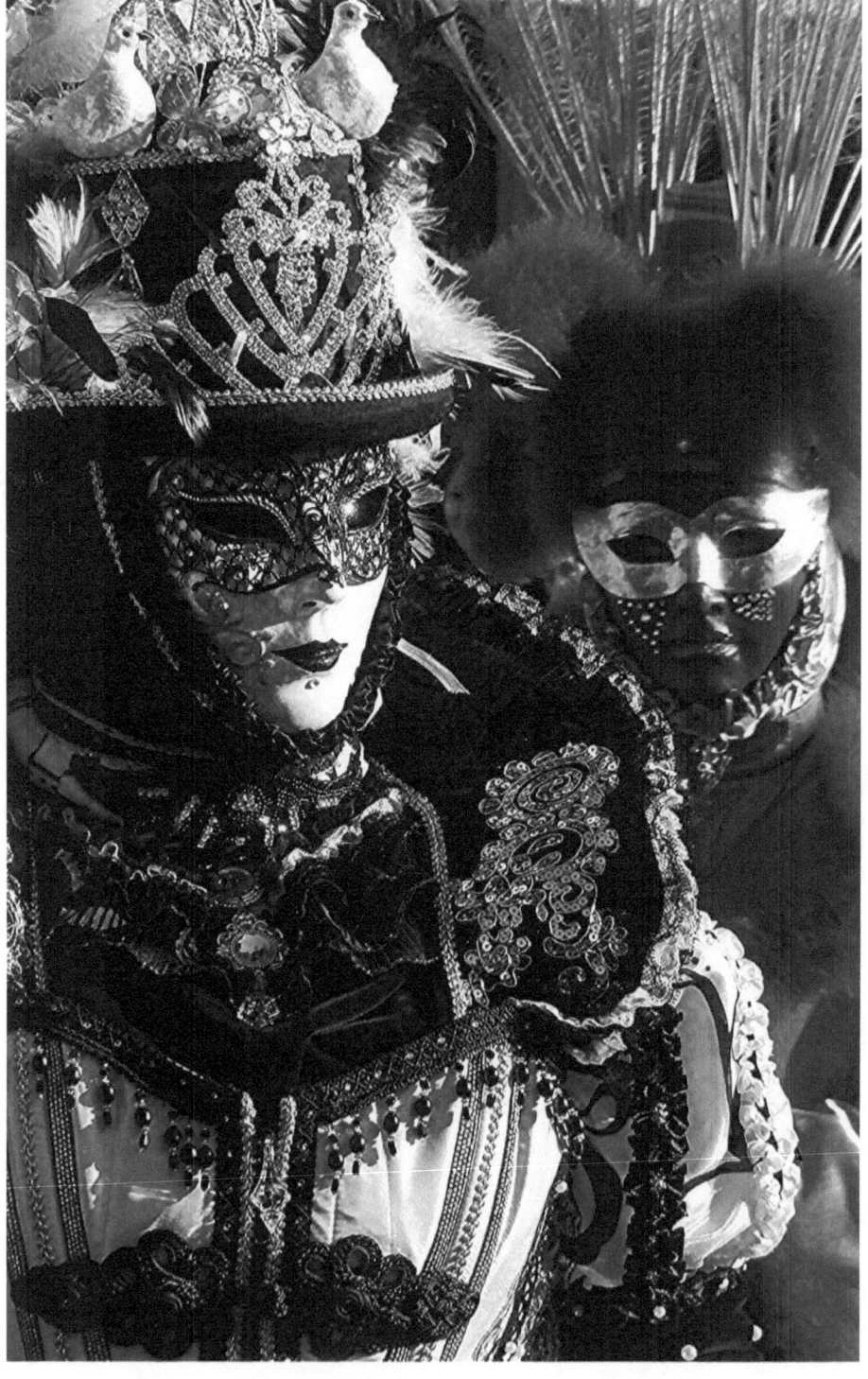

So Me, So You, So Us

My life is through,
Touch the Sky.
Devil loves me too,
And it's time to die.

Walk dry through the fountain,
Through the sky of dark red blue.
To adore the fallen mountain,
I'm nothing without you.

Dead with no spark,
It was never true.
So lonely, so dark,
It's so you.

Darkness cries in soul's faint light,
Fire freezes my blackened heart.
I'm a rotting corpse at midnight,
Lord walking death and his art.

Worship the latest crisis,
Look deep into my mind.
Kiss cold mighty Isis,
Fuck the Heavens blind.

The end of the show,
Nothing to see.
Kill the rainbow.
It's so, so, me.

The king poisons the queen,
A curse with every breath.
Never mind the philistine,
She's the closest thing to death.

Such a weary fool,
Such complicated fuss.
It's so cruel,
It's so us.

Elliott Stein

In this life, I am a baby of the 21st Century.

To wander the crass commercial swirl 'tis my destiny.

My mother's milk is 99% coffee, I suckle the caffeine teat.

I am wired and awake and with hell in my heart I discover...

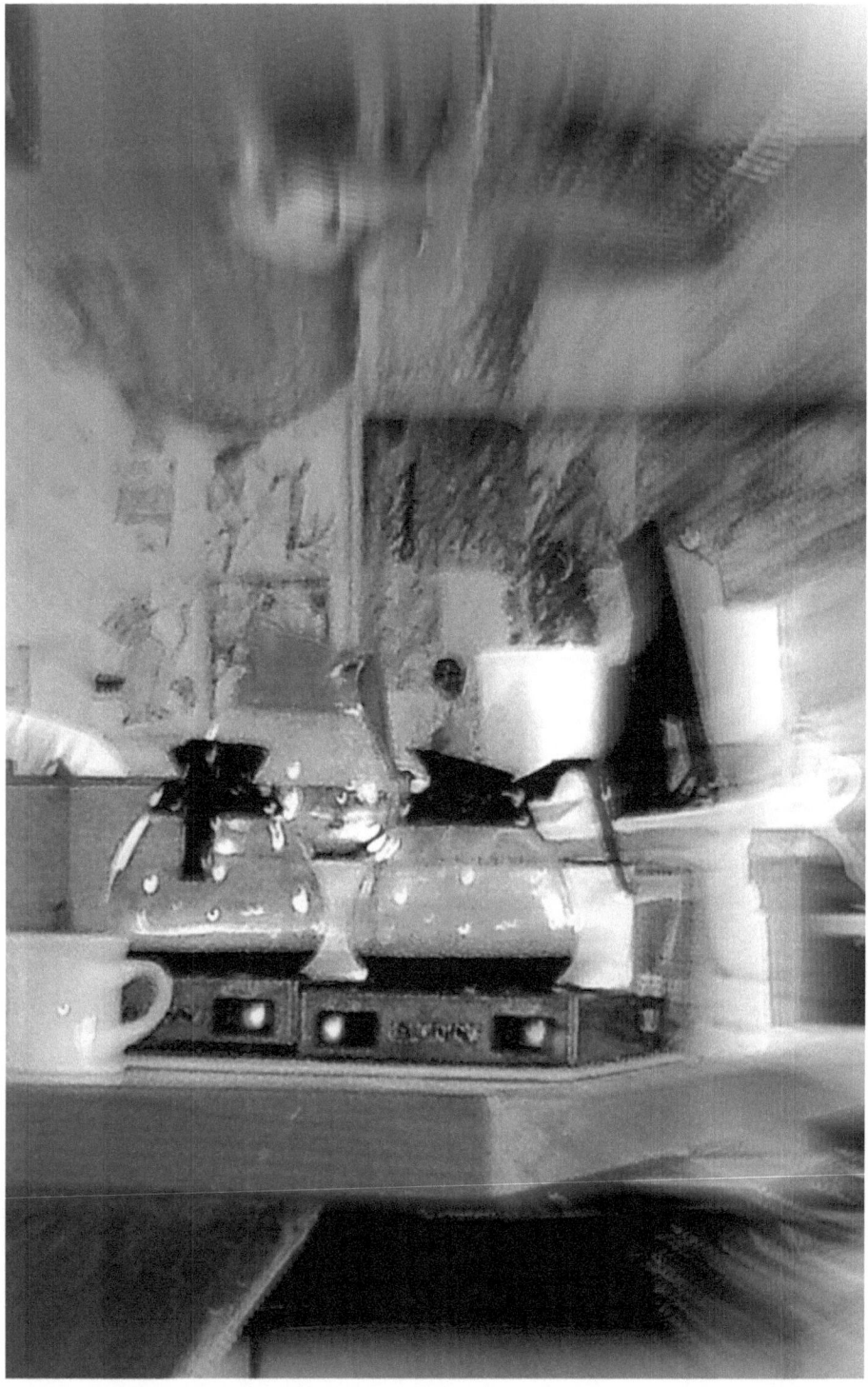

Starbucks Oblivion

A new Starbucks was built,
On an ancient Indian burial ground.
The spirit of the great Navajo,
Raindances in a caffeine fog.

Pop's soda shop is also a Starbucks,
Mom and Pop were bought out.
Their retirement is spent wide-eyed,
On a geriatric cappuccino high.

The County Hospital is no more,
Replaced by something necessary: a Starbucks.
No more police station, school or church,
Now there's Starbucks, Starbucks and Starbucks.

There are no more citizens,
The town is deserted, not a soul in sight.
Just rows and rows of Starbucks,
But no-one to drink the coffee.

Black, no sugar, no milk – nothing.

Past, present, future and never-were undistinguished, as I bring it all to mind – I am there.

Moments crystalize in an eternity, stretched through many lifetimes, and before the space of a first breath.

I am in the forest again, her hand is in mine. I look into her eyes.

The handfast.

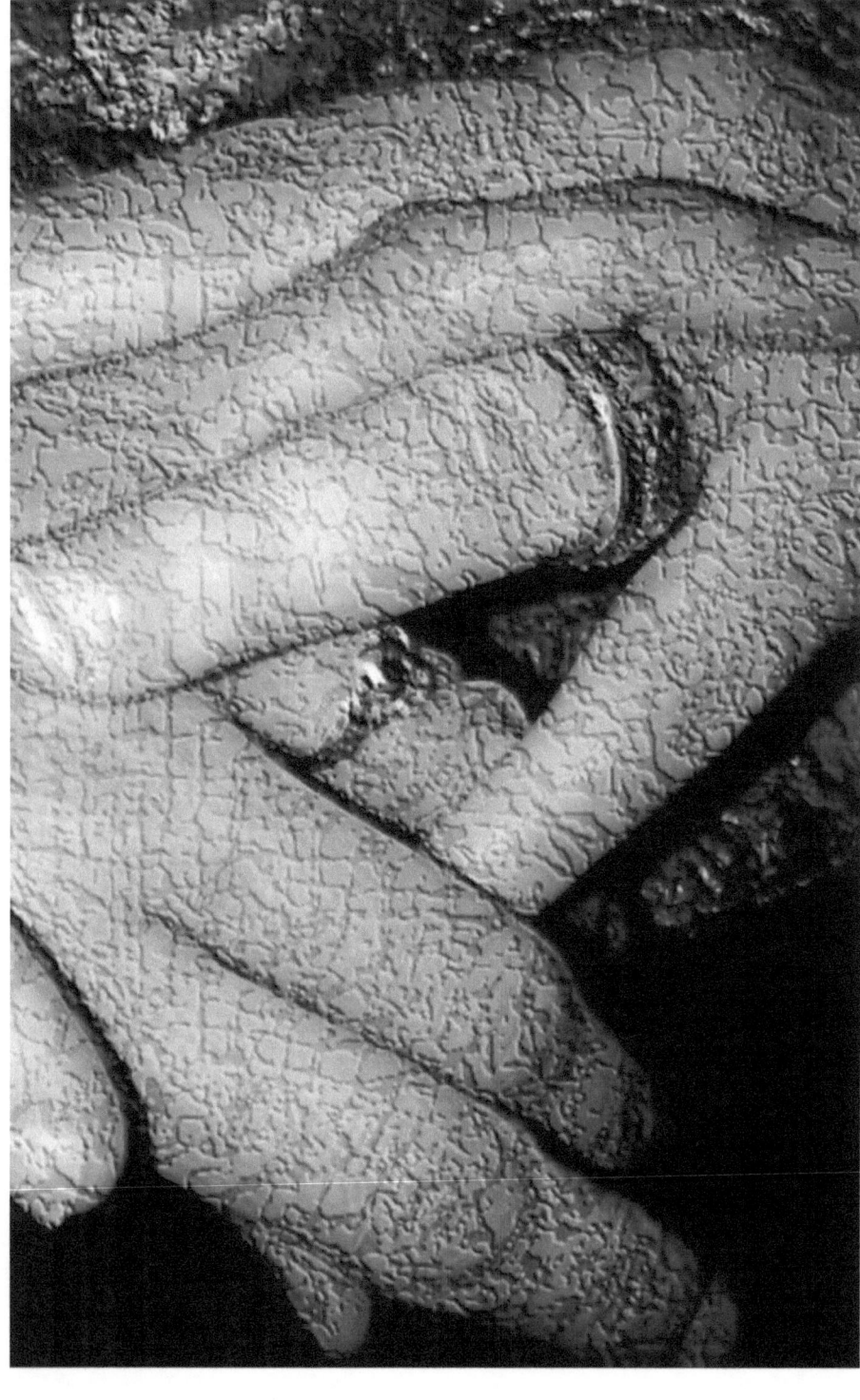

Handfast

Handfast,
A feeling,
At the end of time,
When we're together.

Only a heartbeat away,
Yet eons till we're one again.
An eternity less we part,
The love that fills the void.

From the center of heart,
Comes my word.
I whisper it to you alone,
To feel its intensity.

A creation of power,
Within depths of my soul.
From the universe.
Only to you.

I am a could-be, would-be, hero.

Blazing Heaven is at my heels.

Though just born, I'm living in so many lives. Overwhelmed am I by memories from the other births, and deaths, and all the in-betweens.

It is all so ... real.

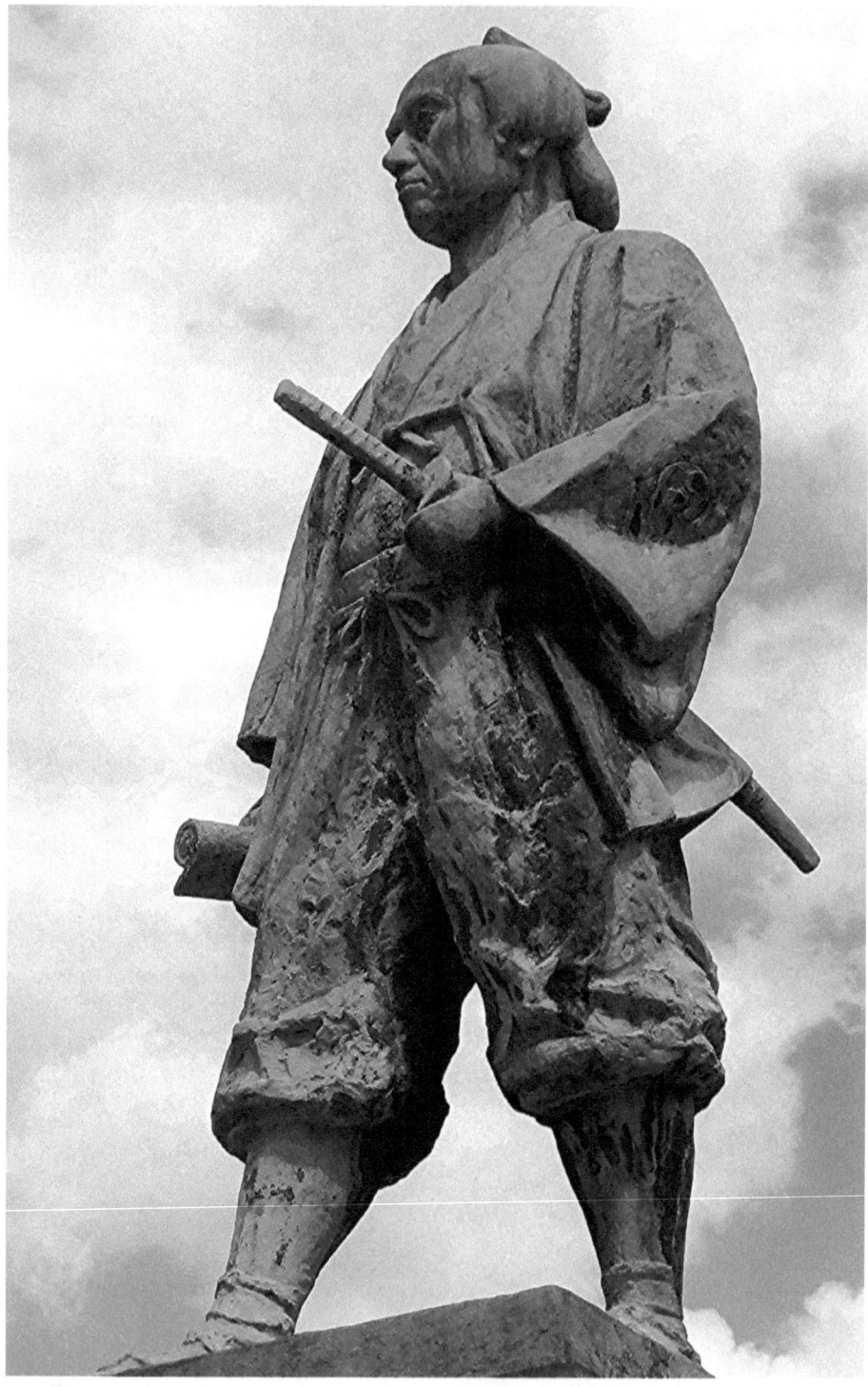

The Magic Scribble

The Magic scribbled,
On the back of the ancient envelope,
Contained a secret message from the heart,
To a stranger dead so long ago.

The prized object of esteem on the mantle,
Of proud victories of another life line,
Stacked in the dusty dirt cheap bargain bin,
Of a nameless antique shop in Anywhere.

In my life my most valued is nothing,
The gold is dust in my soul's eternal.
In the end all that was real is illusion,
Though neverwas tis special and unique.

I require a petty
obsession to distract from a
life of significance.

I desire a distraction from
contemplating the meaning
of a meaningless universe.

Where no meaning exists, I
made one up.

I needed a problem.

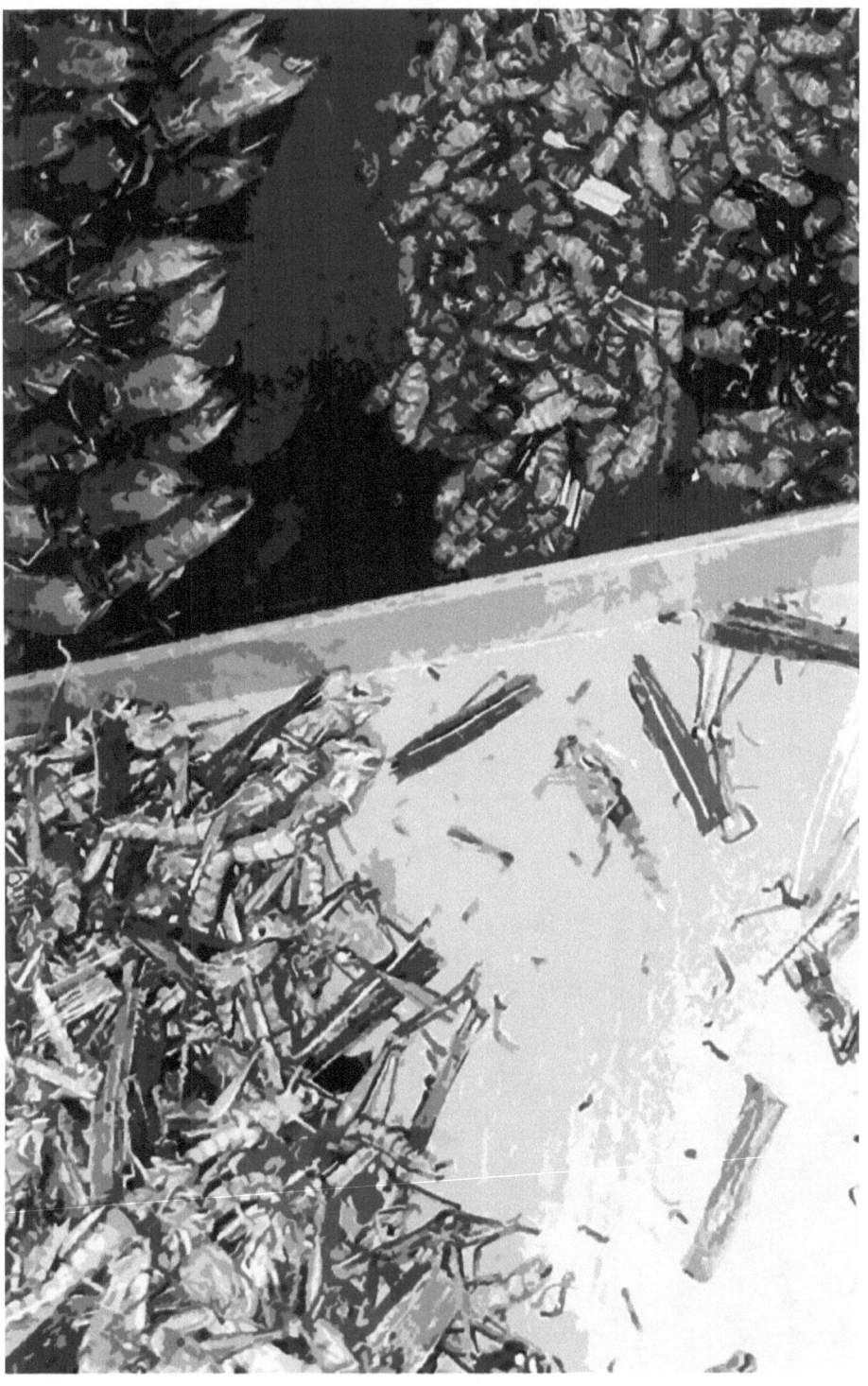

Dead Bug On My Toast

I couldn't finish my breakfast today,
I couldn't eat another bite.
I didn't know what to say,
I just lost my appetite.

I couldn't eat anymore,
Because I finally saw:
A dirty big bug on my toast,
You know the way I feel.
I'm not blaming the host,
If I did I'd be a heel.

The tea was divine,
The sausage tasty and hot.
The eggs turned out fine,
I enjoyed them a lot.

But then came my bread,
With butter and jam on a plate.
When I saw it I saw red,
'Cause there's nothing more I hate.

Than a bug on my toasted bread,
I assumed the bugger was dead.
A dead bug on my toast,
A well done insect roast.
What else can I say?
I've nothing more to boast.
Can't just flick it away,
The dead bug on my toast.

I must numb from my
latest trivial phobia.

I'm too terrified to really
experience pain. Should that
pain in my heart expand, I
might not be able to hold it
together.

Nothing to do but drink
whiskey, the blue label, in
the Electric Blue Suede.

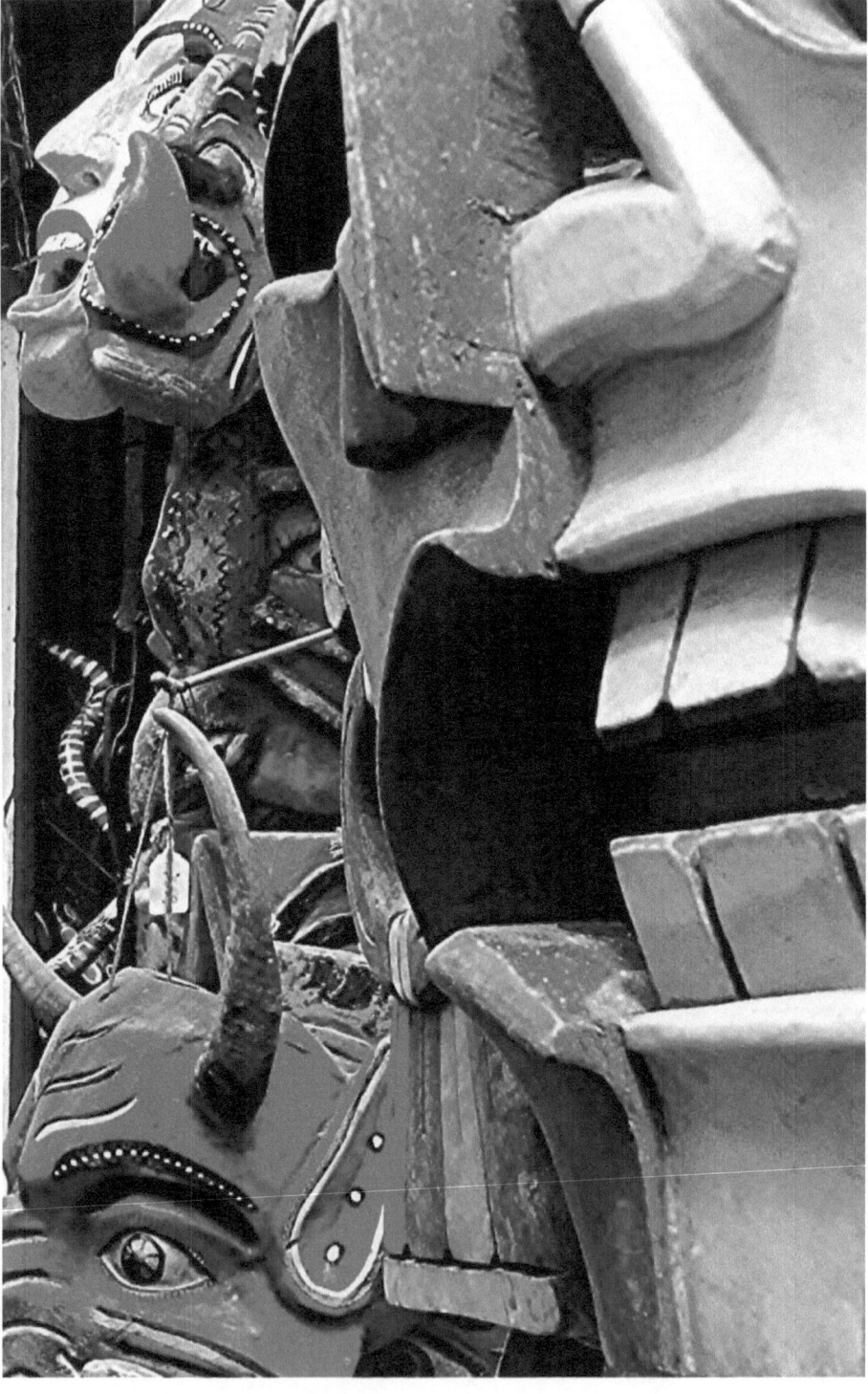

Electric Blue Suede

Burning time by the hours,
Rehearsing what to say.
Listening to the powers,
Reliving another yesterday.

Remembering what the dancer said,
As she fell from the lighted stage.
"There's no more music in my head,
So I'll never be filled with rage."

Electric Blue Suede,
You were life.
We were never paid,
But didn't carry a knife,
Electric Blue Suede.

While others play the game,
And twist reality into lies.
In awe of the flame,
She finally breaks down and cries.
Electric Blue Suede.

I finally stopped from keeping score,
It doesn't matter how many times you've been laid.
She's in love with a shadow once more,
A phantom in Electric Blue Suede.

I can finally see,
Man we had it made.
Let the bastards be,
In Electric Blue Suede.

With whiskey on my mind, and passion on my breath, I self-indulgently question existence at the Electric Blue Suede.

That's where I met HER.

We were two lies entwined in the sheets.

We were sweating hope,
loving unfulfilled dreams,
nurturing long-languishing
broken hearts...

   ... and regrets... sweet,
sweet, regrets.

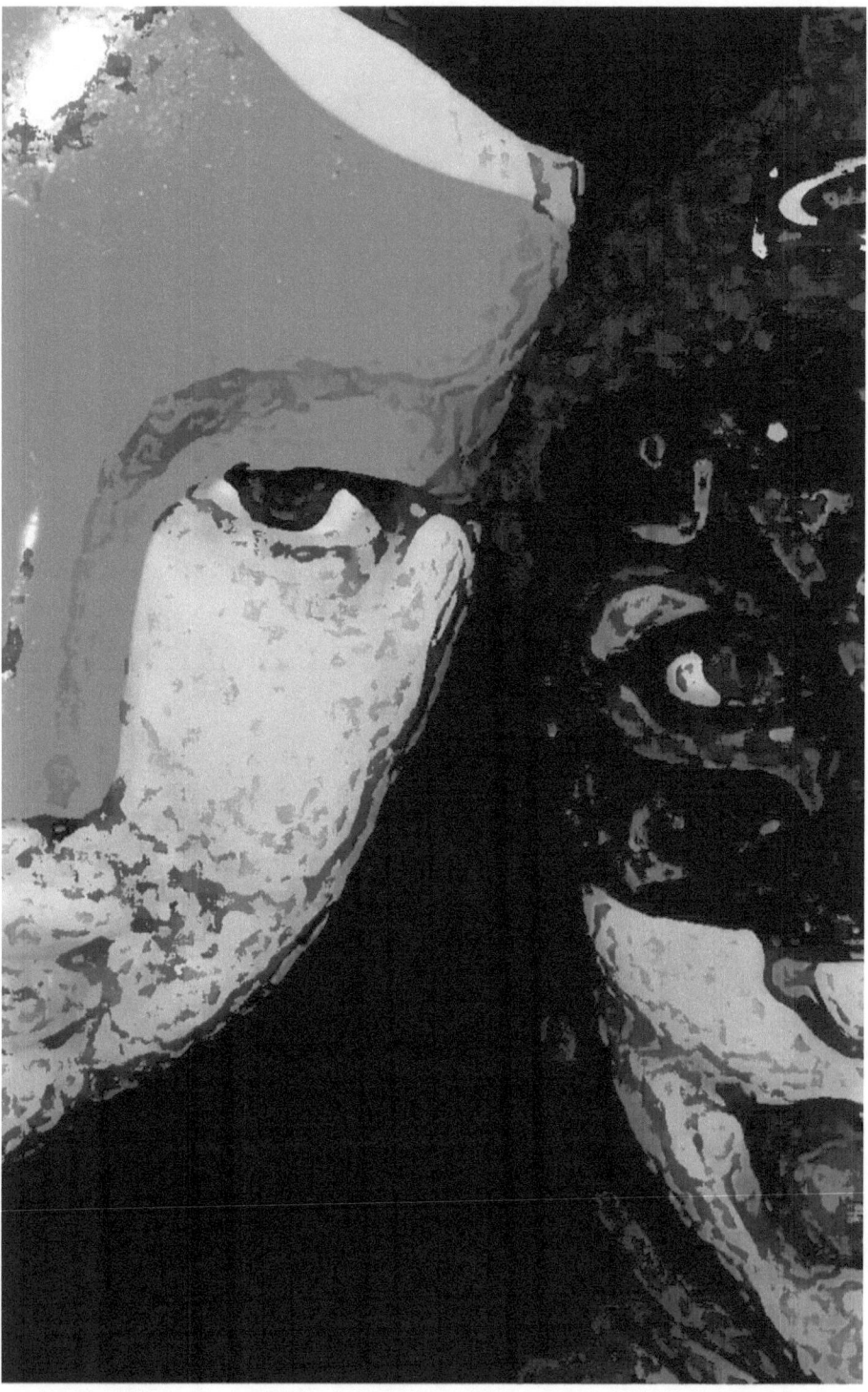

Lovers in Disguise

The sky's always black,
The sun doesn't rise.
I'll never come back,
I'm a lover in disguise.

Your heart's always blue,
I'm the one you despise.
There's no happiness for two,
I'm your lover in disguise.

It doesn't matter if I steal,
Because I'm not real.
If I'm ever nice,
You'll pay the price.
I'm not what you see,
Nothing is free.
And you'll believe all my lies,
'Cause I'm your lover in disguise.

You'd better not be sensitive,
O' gullible fool beware.
I take but never give,
I really, really, don't care.
You'll think you're in bliss,
With my manipulative kiss.

I always do as I will,
It doesn't matter who dies.
It might be you whom I kill,
'Cause I'm a lover in disguise.

Elliott Stein

Numbed Pain: I left
my lover in disguise and
immediately drew up the
defenses.

I only attracted that
which was safe, that which I
could not love, that of which
there was never a risk of
being hurt...

... or of feeling.

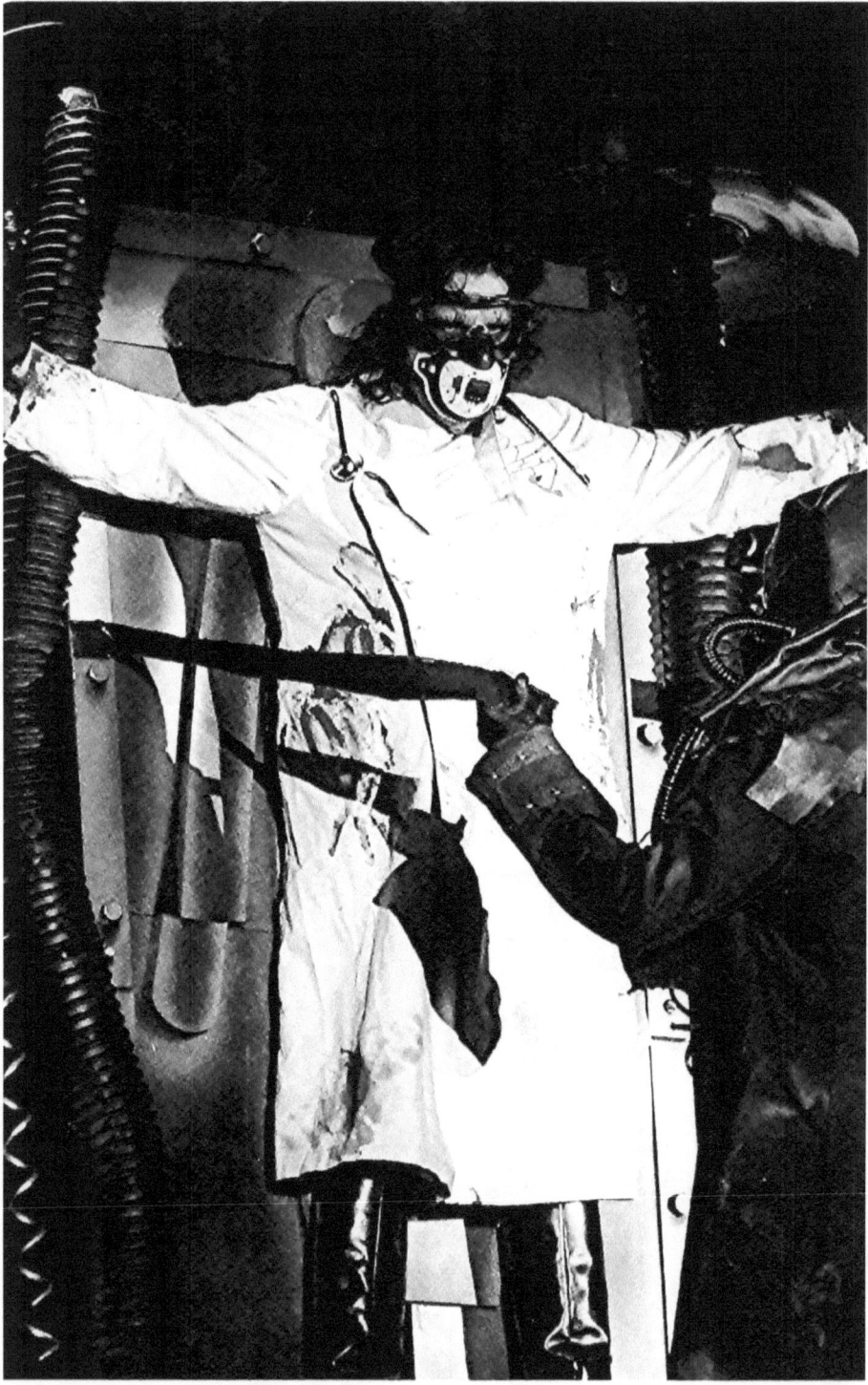

MY TRUE HATE

We could have a happy Life together,
If we didn't hate one-another so.
We'd warm the bed in cold weather,
If I didn't tell you where to go.

My dear, how happy together we'd be,
If you didn't yell "drop dead" on the phone.
If you weren't so repulsed by the sight of me,
We wouldn't have to spend tonight alone.

And we'll never stay out late,
Because it's real true hate.
You'll never tenderly sigh,
'Cause you're praying I'll die.
I'll thank my lucky star,
If you get hit by a car.

You'd be my one and only choice,
And I'd shower you in mink and lace.
If I didn't cringe at the sound of your voice,
And you didn't spit at the sight of my face.

And we'll never buy a house,
Since you think I'm a louse.
Into my arms you'll never swoon,
Because you're such a baboon.
You would so be my wife,
If you weren't such a low life.

Its true hate don't you know,
Walking with one-another fist in face.
Oh my dearest despised we hate us so,
I'm a miserable worm and you're a disgrace.

Elliott Stein

Oh my idiocy!

Completing patterns of my last time wandering, a time when the illusion of power consumed.

I stood as a colossus of an idiot in the physical world, yet so removed was I from my nothingness.

I'll try not to be ashamed
as it's simply how I played
the game.
Don't love the idiot, just
give us your bloody vote.

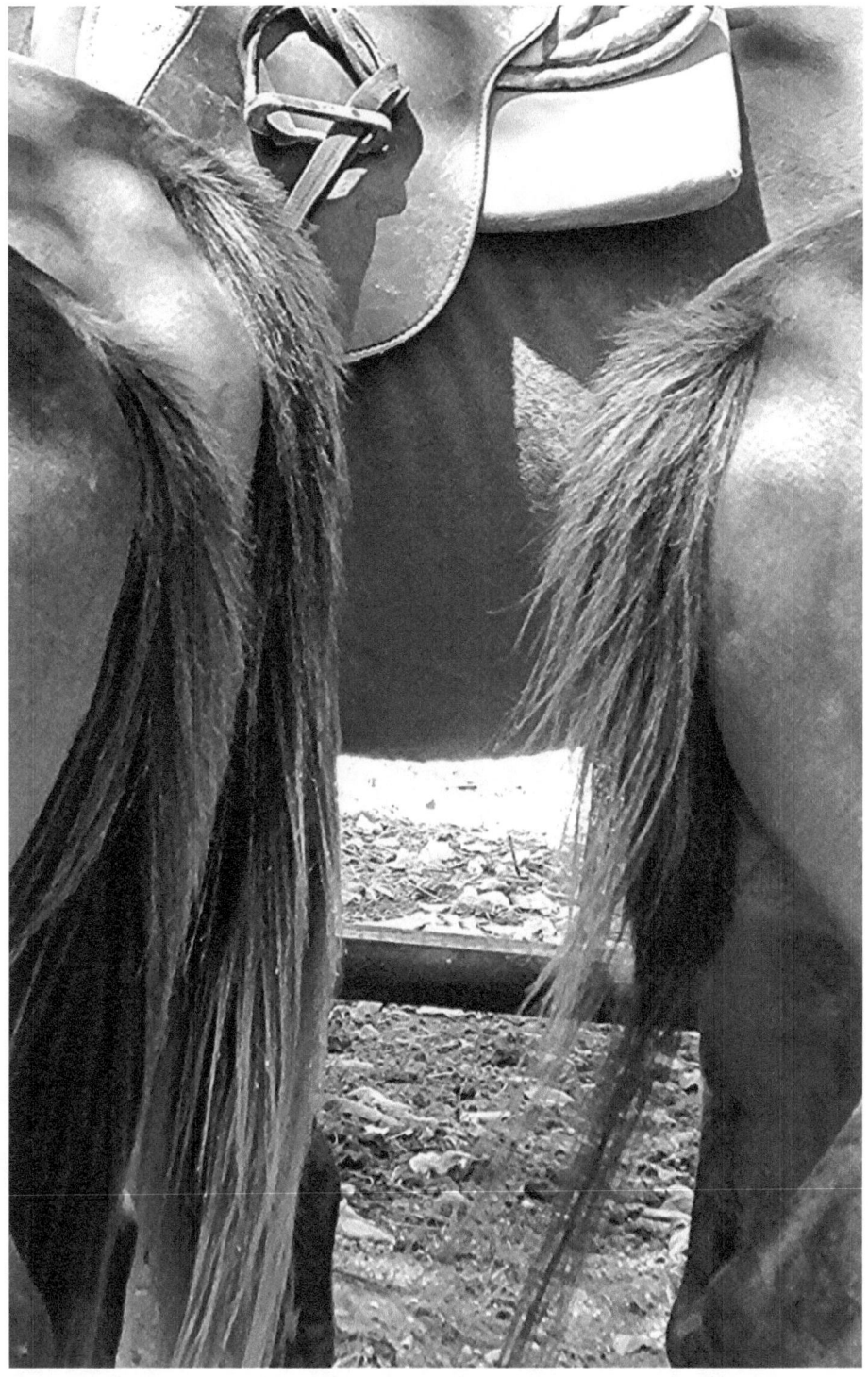

Idiots

Some idiots laugh, giggle and yell 'ping',
Others make laws in Parliament.
Idiots make speeches about everything,
For that's how idiots pay their rent.

Idiots enjoy a position which rules,
And often hold worlds in their idiotic hands.
Surrounded by fellow idiots and fools,
They travel about in idiotic bands.

Though amusing the idiot's a dangerous pest,
So beware of heads which are hollow.
Though their ideas may seem a ridiculous jest,
Other dangerous idiots may follow.

I am not here yet, can't be here yet.

I'm just lying on my back, trapped in a tiny useless body, with eyes that can't focus.

The last lives still haunt me.

My true love waits in the space beyond.

My dearest, I was a fool to leave you for this existence.

It is nonexistence I long for.

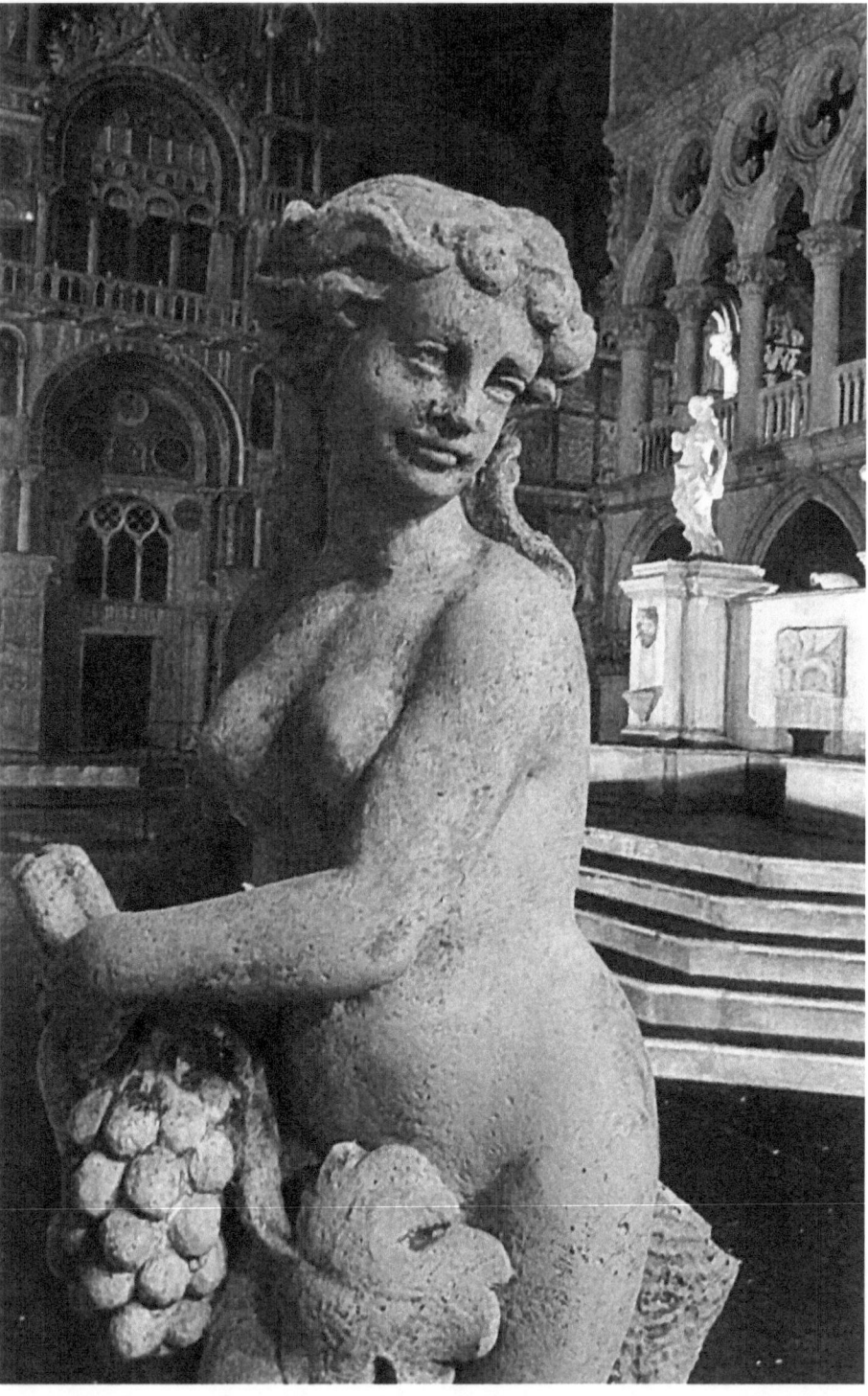

At The End Of Time

I'm waiting for you at the end of the universe.
I'd forgotten you in this body,
But not in my soul.
We're forever in the eternity of our longing dreams.

And when all eyes eventually close,
So tight they are finally open.
And the images of our dreams,
Manifest in the hearts of lovers.

Every new breath,
Elevate the heavens Earthbound.
It gifts soul to soul,
And becomes the Universe.

You are there, I know you are.
I always knew.
Even when lying next to another,
I was waiting just for you.

We created it,
Long ago.
In the beyond within the between,
We're the one divided.

Again, memories of dying
and of being born again.

So many regrets, many
lifetimes of not experiencing
pain where numbness
prevailed.

I tried to discover the
heart by misdirecting it
through my mind.

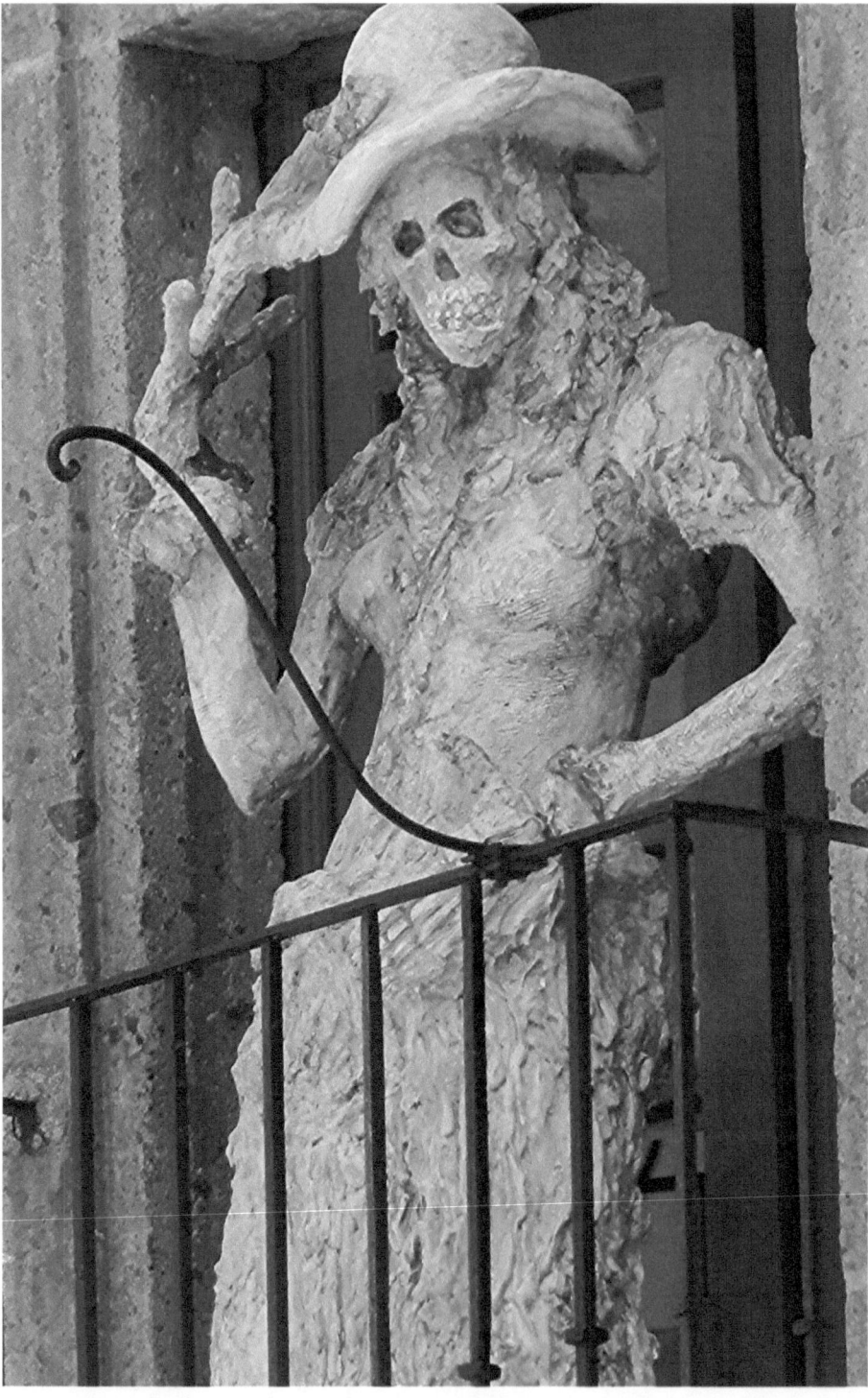

Ever So Brief

Awoke from a forgotten dream,
It wasn't night nor day.
Realized the lion's share of this stream,
Had flowed silently away.

I can feel the end ever so near,
There is no hate in my heart.
There are no lovers and no fear,
No nothing, no ending, yet no start.

Soured fears of fragmented tears,
The trains departed come not this way.
Another life before me appears,
Another reflection of yesterday.

I slept ever so briefly,
No longer a desire to scream.
All the memories faded quickly,
Awoken another forgotten dream.

Everything from limbo to think,
Nothing in the Universe to say.
Before I could even blink,
Yet another life slipped away.

I can feel the end ever nearing,
There is not surrender nor fight.
There is numbness and there's feeling,
There is darkness and there's light.

Elliott Stein

Do who you remember who I used to be?

I thought that identity would be immortal. Perhaps a statue of me would be built.

Those were hopeful dreams of a nobody.

Not many people think of me, few even remember that identity.

Nothing about me comes up in a Google search.

If I'm not Googled - did I really exist?

All the objects of recognition are gone and now recognize someone else.

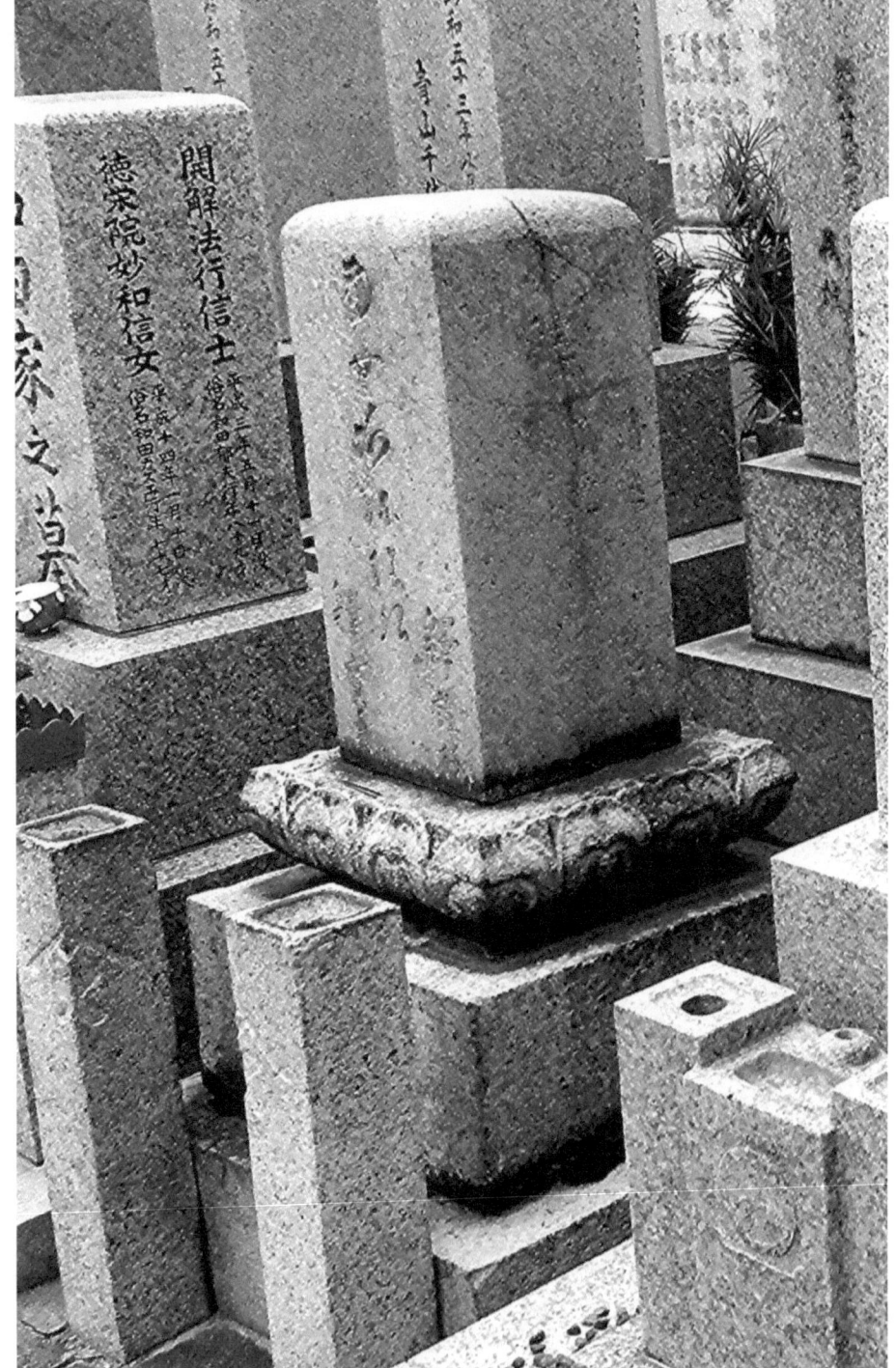

Legion Of The Nameless.

Everything turns to dust so quickly.
My life's work is filed away in a cabinet,
And pulped with all the other papers.
The gold of my soul returns to the Earth.

All the photos and souvenirs from holidays long ago,
Are in an old cardboard box of useless tat for sale.
Tossed in with other grubby forgotten artifacts,
Of the dusty forgotten faceless like me.

My children barely remember me by now,
One of them remembers the month my birthday was in.
Grandchildren only know me as concept,
Not as a flesh and blood man.

There are a few vague stories occasionally
exchanged about me,
Every once in a while someone raises a glass to my memory.
And then I vanish into history again,
And join the legion of the nameless.

In many lives there is one
fixed location in the fluid
points of time.

There is a room in every
lifeline that I spent on this
plane where I reconnect with
all my past and yours.

A pilgrimage to Paris, and queue for the Louve, to just sit in the Richelou Statue room.

Staring and peacefully connecting.

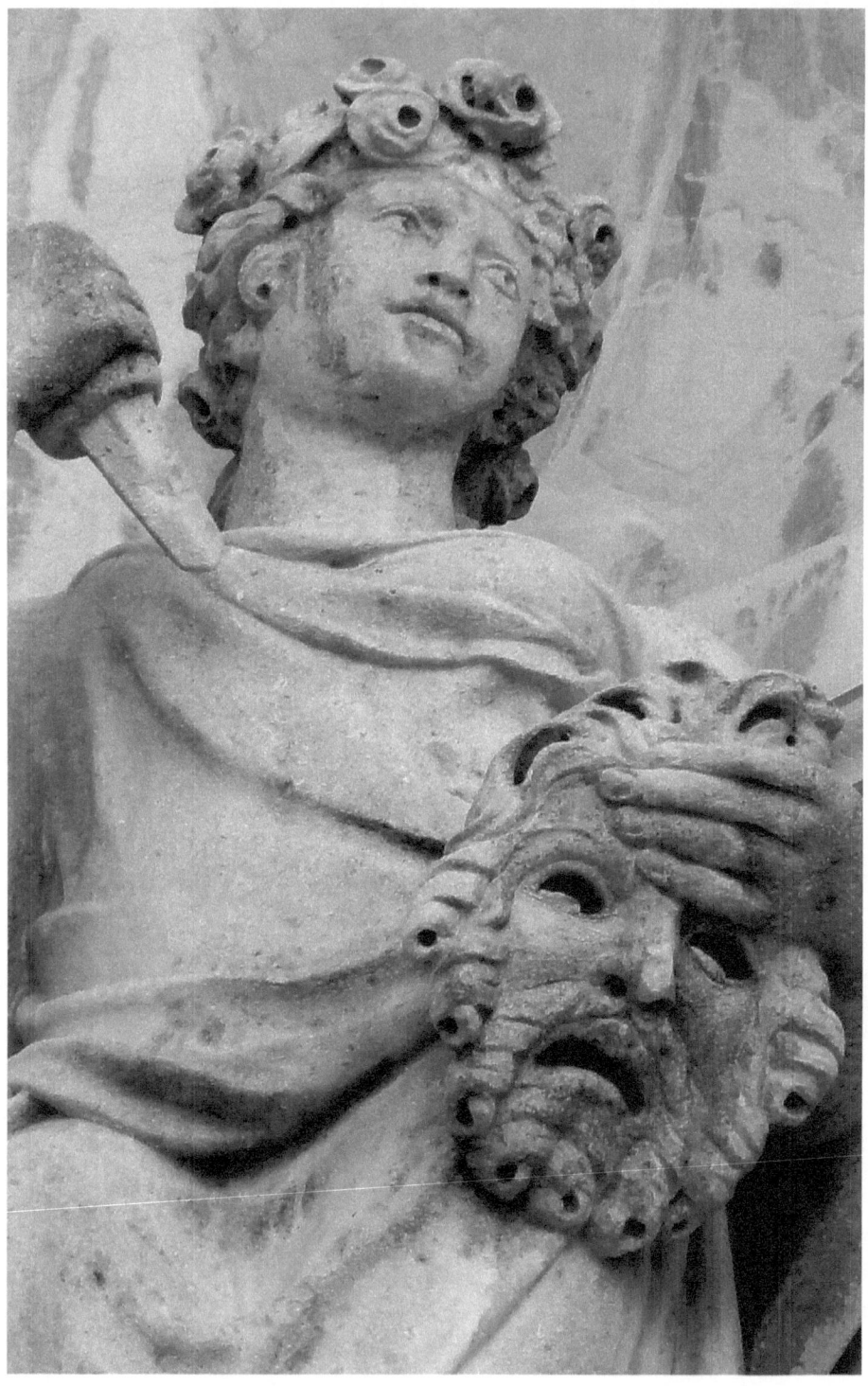

Poem to the Richelou Statue Room- Louve Fri Jan 2001

The joy of completing this life,
And moving onto the construct.
Limitless in time,
Limitless in imagination.

To create where I am at this second,
At any instant of my bidding.
To have you and only you,
In this palace of unrivaled beauty forever.

Amongst the stone people so cold, so alive,
Impassioned by years of love and toil by creators long gone.
These timeless beauties of the never living souls,
Would watch us; would protect us,
Would be the backdrop of love neverending.

This castle would be ours,

The students with charcoal and paper would be in their time.

Our time would stand still near the

green titans at the entrance,

Under the open glass sky where time stands still,

And love breathes through grand designs eternal.

Elliott Stein

Trapped in the illusionary reality.

In that big world, in that past life, this small man needed to prove himself.

The world couldn't discover the secret of my smallness.

They need to know I made it, at what-ever cost, to the even smaller man.

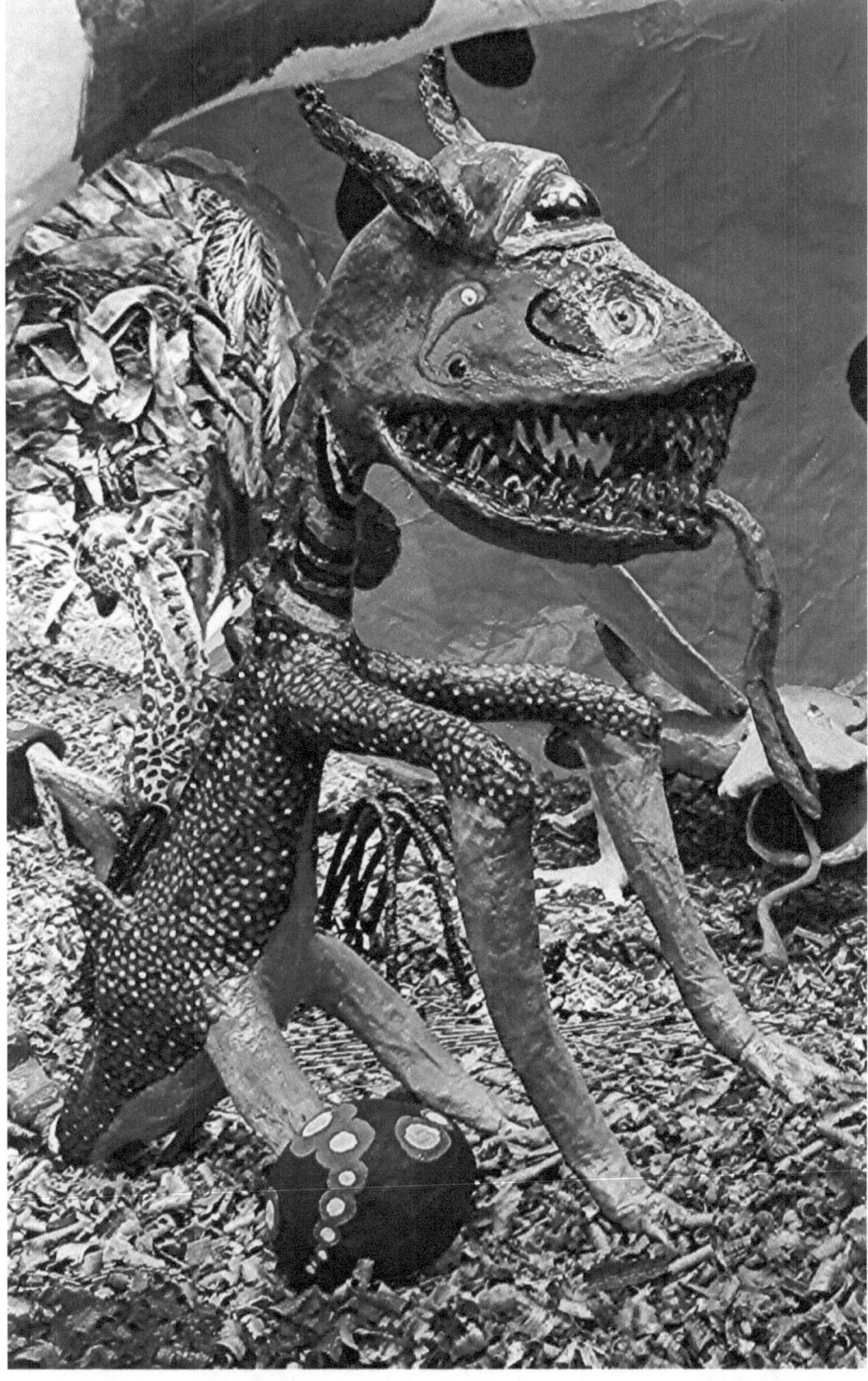

The Small Man

Do you remember the small man,
Who was unhappy and blue?
The one who always ran,
Is now doing something new.

Do you remember the small man,
Who was never quite right?
The one we had to ban,
Because he didn't choose to fight.

Guess what happened to the small man,
The one so different from us?
He became his biggest fan,
And left on a bus.

The pathetic small guy,
Turned out to be a secret wiz.
You'll probably want to cry,
Now that the last laugh is his.

That small man had to eat, had to survive, had to pay a mortgage, had to feed my wife and kids, and have my green lawn be envied.

I played the corporate game and all it cost was IO pieces of my soul.

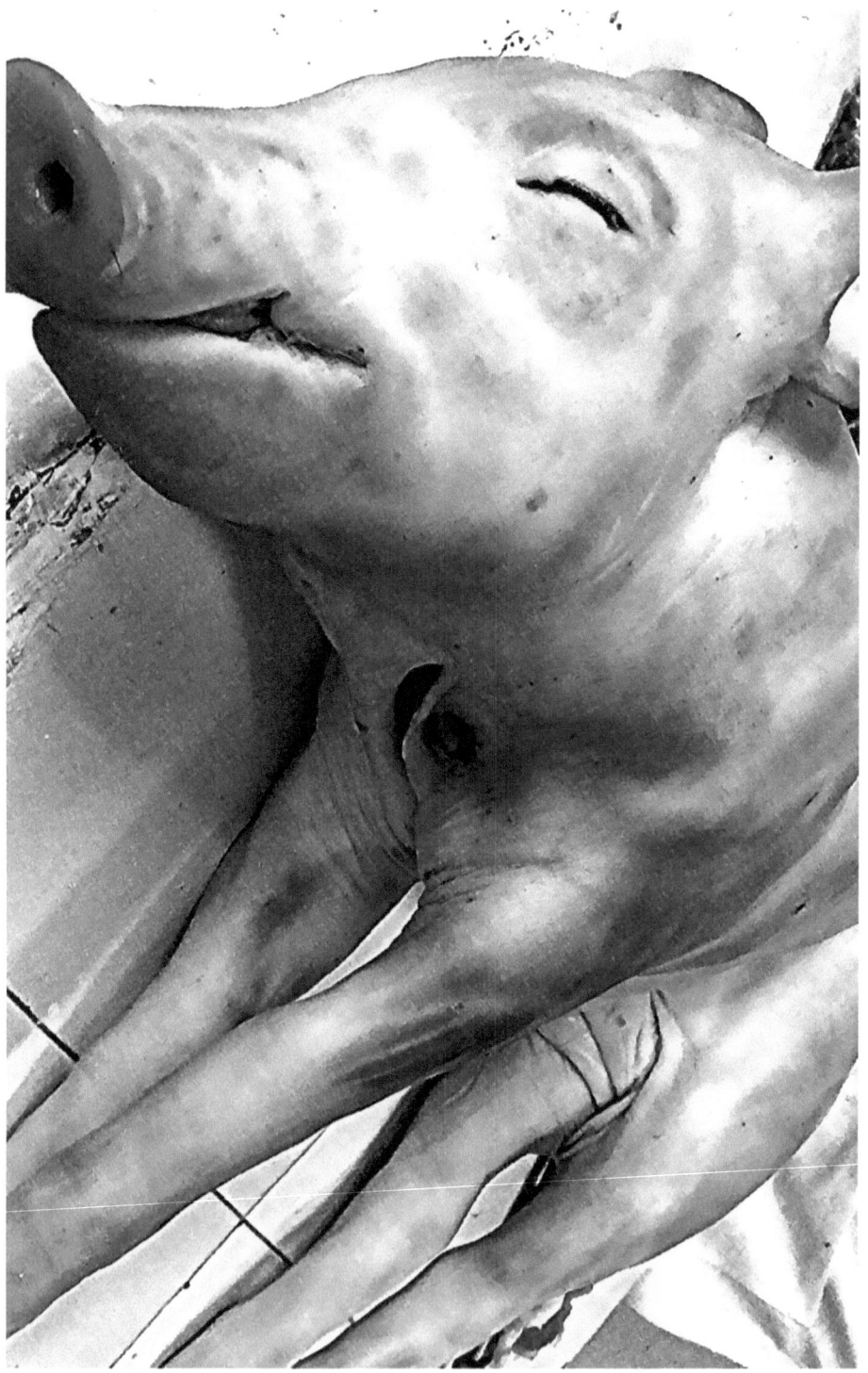

Corporate On My Knees

Hal has the flesh sucker blues,
And spends too much time on his knees.
Desperately sucking the corporate line,
His survival depends on mouth explosions.

David is a brown nosed superstar,
Ass prints on his face match the company tie.
The putrid smell of the company logo,
Reflect a life that lives the big lie.

Laura's two beefy plump ones,
And walking marketing between the legs.
With wetness as a networking tool,
She sleeps every inch to the top.

The corpses run the whole muther,
With fluid exchange but no power at top.
White protein trickles down to the masses,
And the bastards choke on it all day long.

I had built an empire of
illusion. I possessed such
good symbols of making it.

Had the partner, had the
car, had all those fucking
t-shirts.

And the more I got, the
more I hated it.

I needed to burn it all.

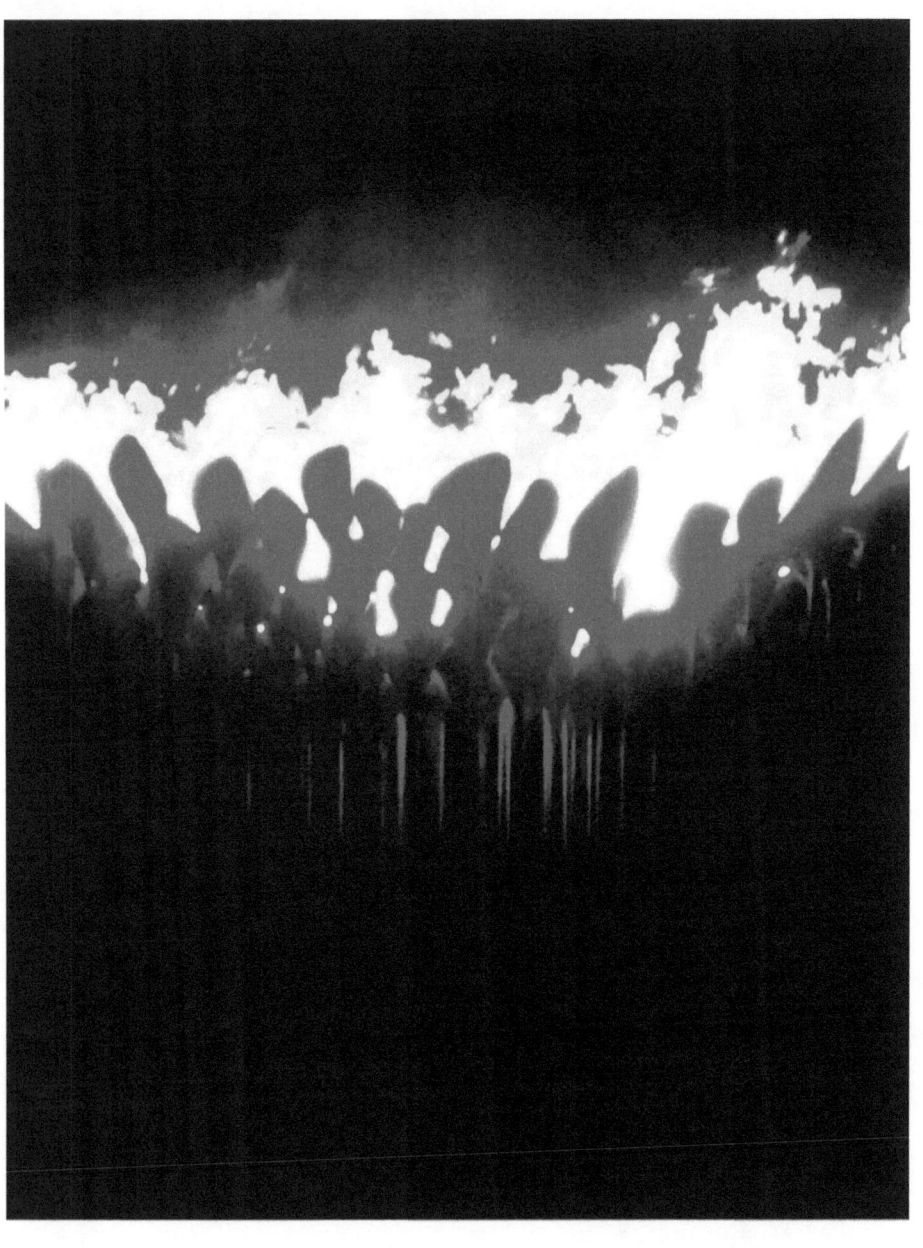

Burn It All

Foolish as I would be,
I just want to burn all of it.
Blight the beauty I once beheld,
Disgrace the pride I once felt.

I want to tear it all down:
The respect and esteem I once built.
Turn my back on the great love of my life,
And crawl to a miserable corner.

Where there once stood a tall hero,
Is a fallen flawed disappointment.
The soul once committed to a world,
Now darkly defends from imaginary foes.

I want to hide,
In the shadows,
As a wounded animal,
And die.

Burning and tearing was
too painful to bear, my heart
raced so, my skin so tight.

With a sense of false
control, I was in the skin of
a groveling, toadying, twit.

The world, for a brief
moment, made sense...

And then didn't.

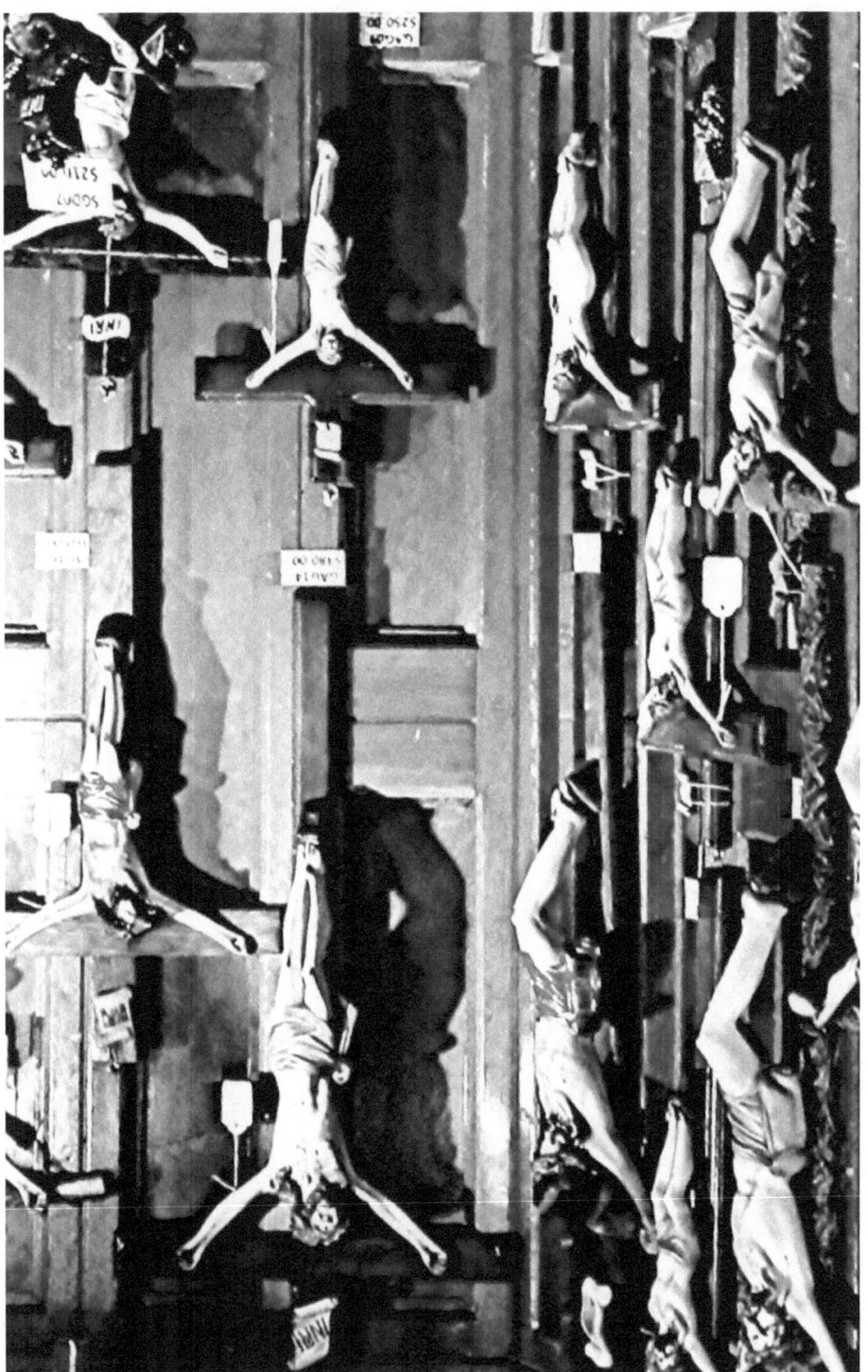

Twits

Twits come in all sizes, colours and IQ,
Twits lead a very silly type of life.
Twits can be cheerful, unhappy or blue,
Twits can be single or with husband or wife.

Twits can blunder a financial decision,
Or build things which later collapse.
Twits make a mockery of the art of precision,
As they wander with a memory lapse.

To stand proudly in the annals of twitdom,
Bungling, failing and falling about.
Wreaking havoc throughout the kingdom,
Spreading airs of uncertainty and doubt.

"A twit in the hand has the IQ of President Bush",
A saying of twits from Downing Street to Westminster.
Spoken by the idiot with the most ridiculous mush,
The silly twit who became the Prime Minister.

So this twit closed his
eyes and created noise in my
head so I didn't have to hear.
And in that dark racket
came a moment of clarity.
Fear so fearful there is
but numbness.

To live in a post 9/11 fog, in a land of illusionary freedoms, with a government's hand up imaginary terrorist's backs.

Pulling strings to the loyal but duped pawns...

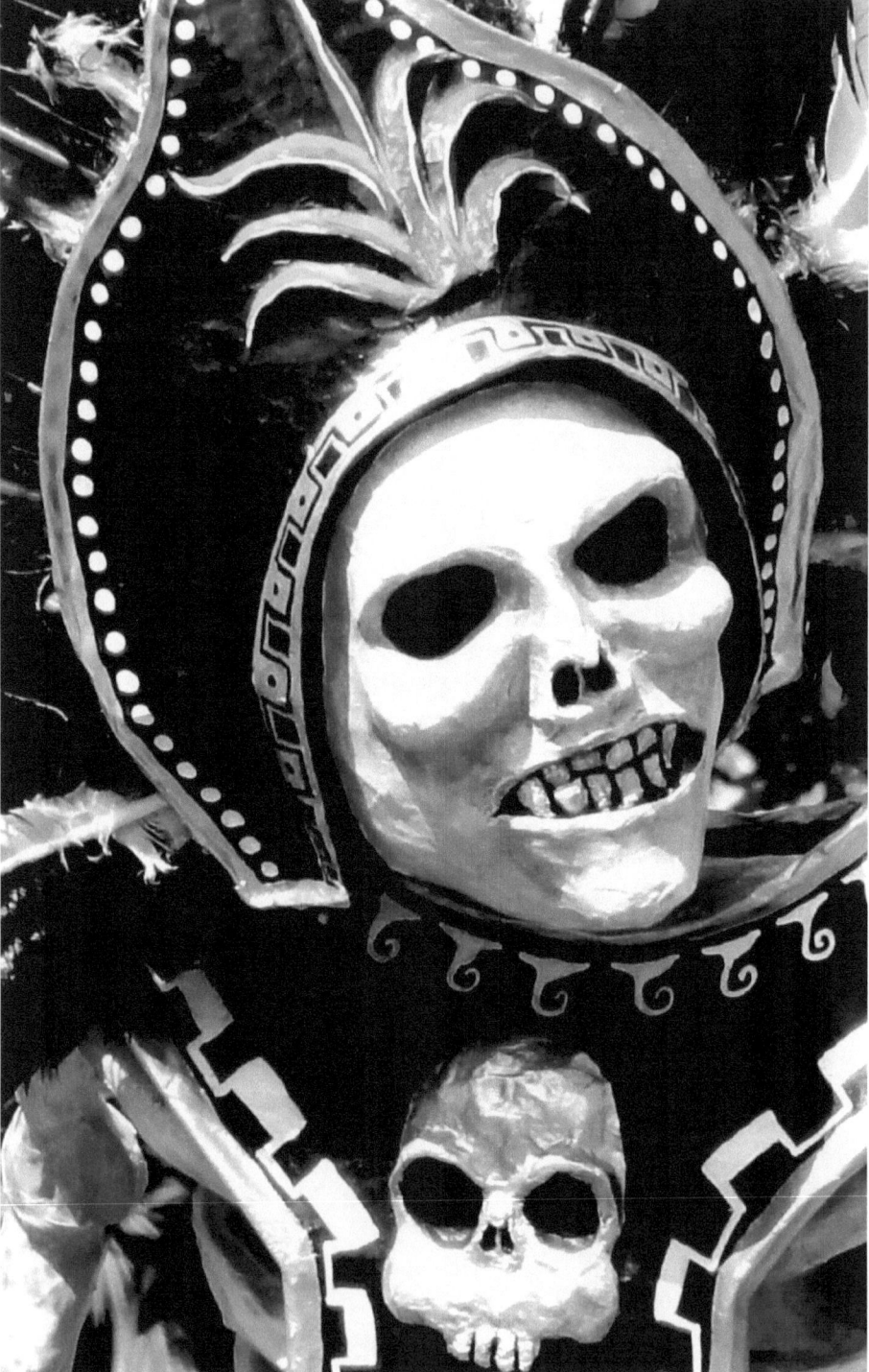

All American Fool

You're my brave all American fool,
Confused by what they taught you in school.
My heroic all American klutz,
Oh middle class suburban putz.

Stroll past while the peasants drown in the pool,
Because you're my heartless, brave, all American fool.

You'll make many sacrifices,
For the sake of rising prices.
Join the army and march to war,
To protect your proud and polluted shore.

In your uniform made by mass production,
Paid for by political corruption.
You'll fight for whatever bureaucracy rules,
Cause you're one of the many all American fools.

You'll protect me from the terrorist invasion,
You'll defend each and every civil right.
(The ones we still have)
You'll proudly hold the flag for capitalism,
You won't give up without a fight.

You'll stand tall and proudly say,
That I fight for the American way.
You'll defend the increasing national debt,
By defeating the imaginary terrorist threat.

You'll learn to be crude and cruel,
'cause you're my heartless, brave,
All American fool.

Elliott Stein

As buildings fell, I saw the REAL villains frame actors.

I was fearful of a secret renegade government. There was real fear of imaginative conspiracies.

The world has gone mad, puppets are elected, and power rests all below in those above.

To The Victims and the
other real victims, the ones
nobly trapped in a lie.

In serving what they
believe is right, betrayal
by such a high source is too
inconceivable to conceive.

The lie is fed.

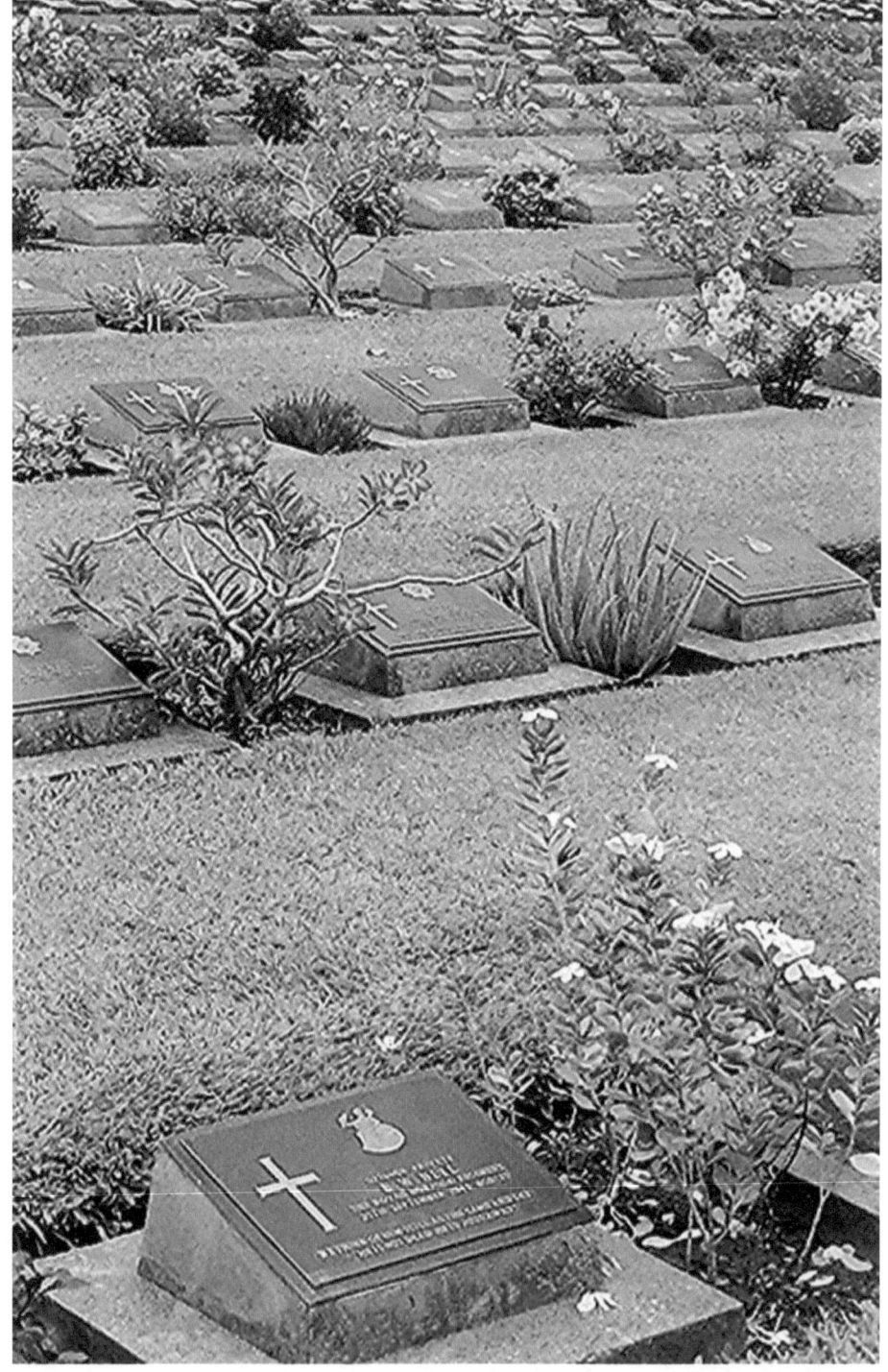

Military Men From The Doomsday Opera

We're waiting for our orders.
We're all military men,
All here to die when,
We get our orders.

We're taught to win a fight,
We're trained to kill on sight.
Our swords defeat mighty pen,
Because we're military men,
Waiting for our orders.

We pretend we're to defend,
As we're waiting for the end.
You might call us insane,
As death falls from our plane,
If that be our orders.

We know it's all in vain,
We'll all die just the same.
Soon comes the deadly rain,
Soon we play our lethal game,
But that is our orders.

Off we fly… into the valley of death,
Away we go… to draw a final breath.
They've got their bombs… we have our mortars,
It is suicide… but that's our orders.

Elliott Stein

Once upon a time, in the land of the free, I tried to speak.

I spoke wrong though I spoke the truth. I contravened all of the unwritten laws that are in the background and that keep it all together.

I shall be punished.

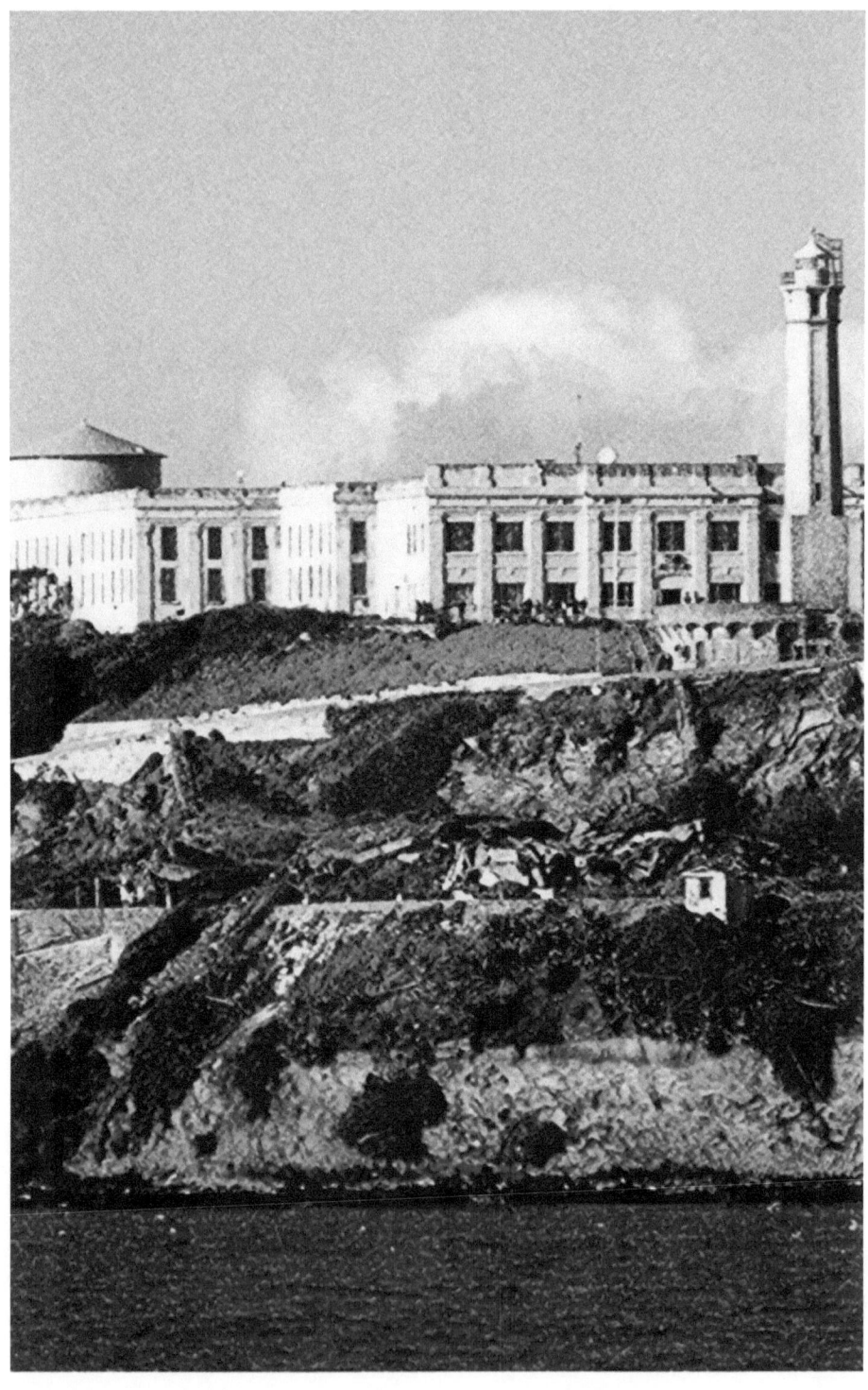

The Courtroom

Guilty in the sea,
Of Human misery.
Guilty before I plead my case,
By the demons who cannot see my face,
In the injustice of all injustice… called justice.

My indisputable evidence matters not,
I'll still be in a prison cell to rot.
The case is so unfairly built,
That I cannot dispute my guilt.
I'm trapped in the injustice of all injustice… called justice.

It's a nightmarish farce of a play,
Designed to keep me locked away.
To imprison my words within a cell,
As I live my living death in this hell.
They're part of the injustice,
That stands high in all injustice… called justice.

The meaning of life lies
in cubes melted on the bottom
of the glass.

It poisons my broken
heart and intoxicates hope.

Thank God for Novocain.
In all its many forms and
thoughts, it truly or falsely
makes the pain go away.

Elliott Stein

I cant feel my heart anymore but at least there is no pain.

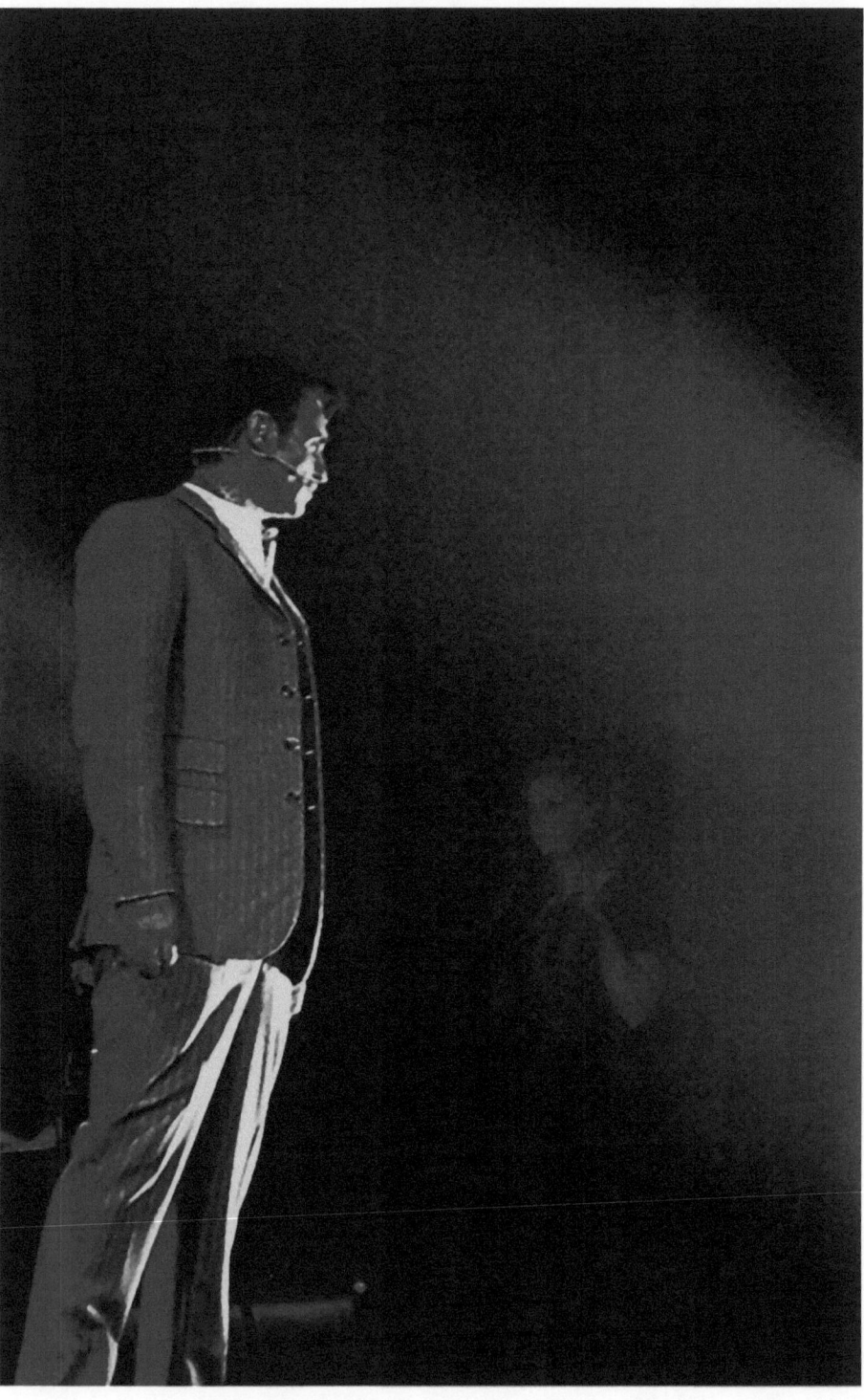

Novocain Dreams

Novocain dreams are painless,
A dose of no cry and no pain.
Darkness radiates through liquid sun,
Clouds pour designer synthetic rain.

No name, I know that stranger well,
A walk through the music of a tear.
Where reality begs to differ,
The brief smoke burns through fear.

A painless dentist laughs at steel,
Laughs down the barriers of soft stone.
Bleed pure white and blue blood soap,
Advertise for a good time all alone.

Numbed to the souls
eyeballs, I submerge into the
real world of illusion.

My past dramas heighten
as yesterday is today.

Professionally laughed at,
professionally ridiculed, I
hide my heart.

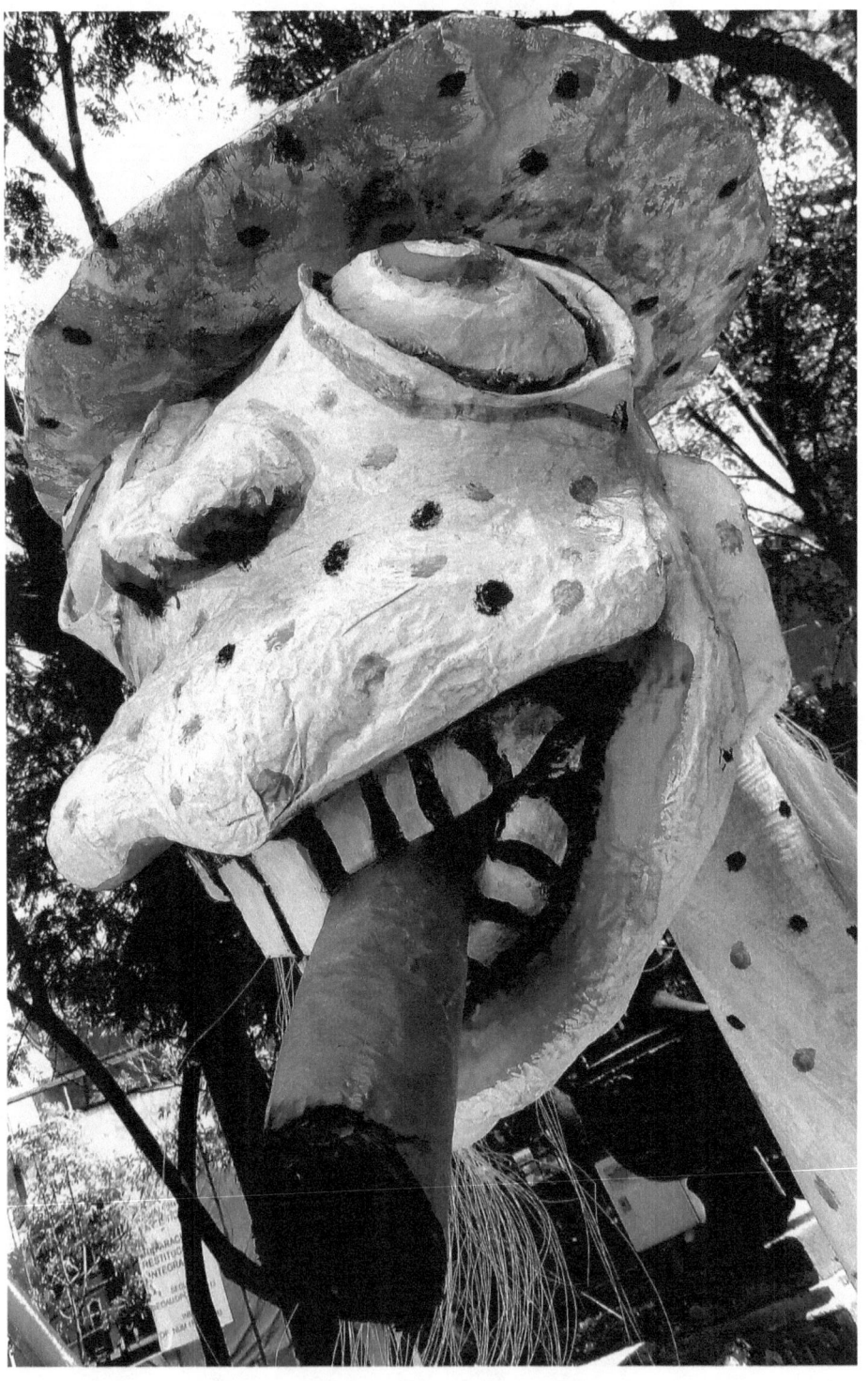

The Clown

Unhappy and sad,
Red drawn frown.
Can never be sad,
I am the clown.

Face painted in white,
The audience is right.
I'm not of flesh and blood,
I take pratfalls in mud.
I can never be down,
Because I am the clown.

Since to the public I'm know,
I only cry when alone.
I'm only a noun,
I am the clown.

Forfeiting my power
to create life, I lingered
through the synthetic
jungle.

I lived and avoided love
in the city of steel and
glass.

I ate my microwave meal
alone and sucked up the
recycled air. As the colour
left my white face, I prepared
for the fight ahead.

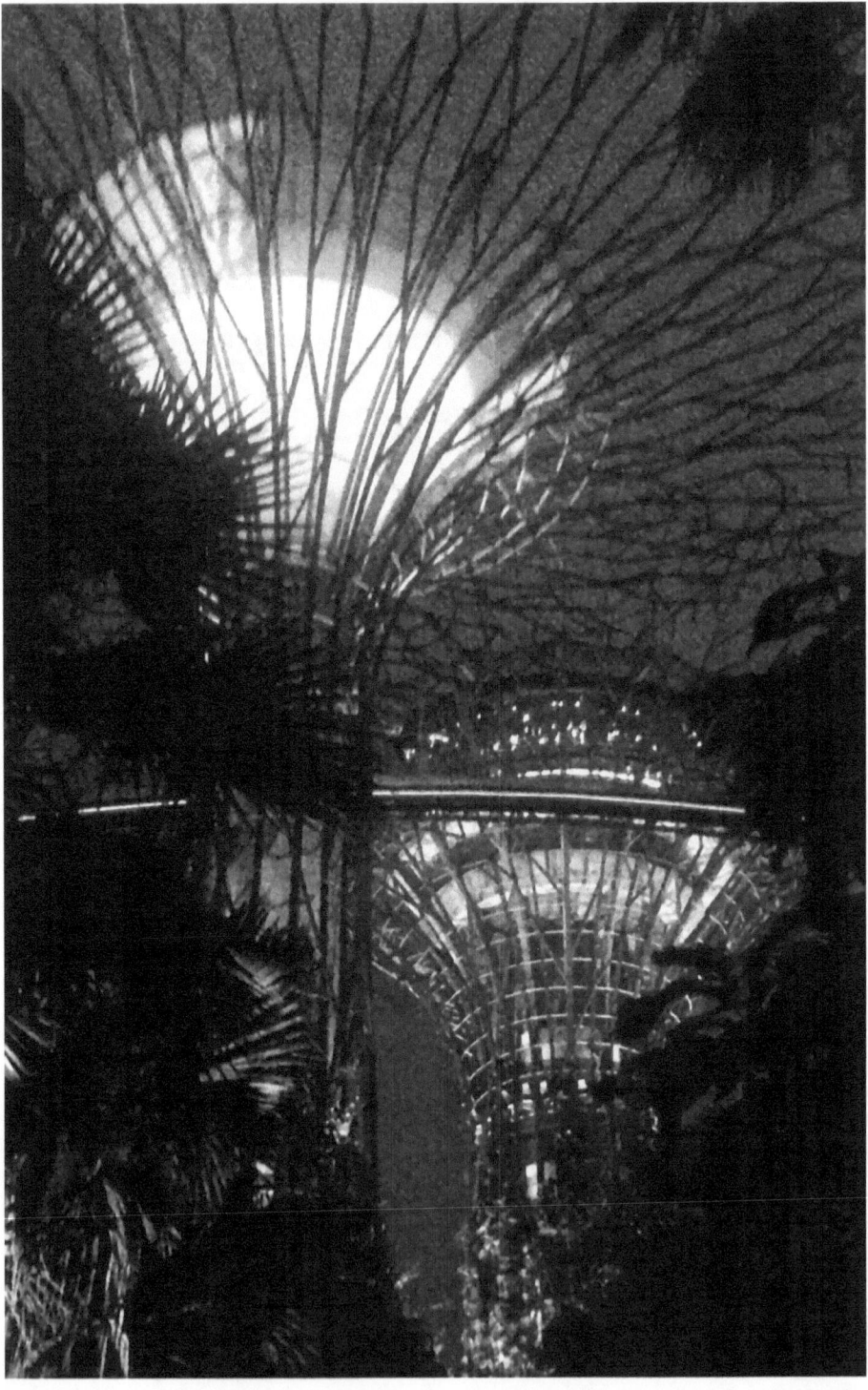

Synthetic Jungle

The metal spider dies,
While crawling on chrome walls.
In search of platinum flies,
Into its aluminum web it falls.

Past the golden mice,
Living on brass floors.
Spreading silver-plated lice,
From its battery operated cores.

Crawling by the steel man,
While embracing his copper wife.
During their crusade to ban,
Their artificial life.

I tried to cut it in the synthetic jungle but the machinery just wouldnt accommodate.

Their gadgets and gizmos rebelled.

The sinister AC/ DC currents attacked, conspired, for my modern mechanical downfall.

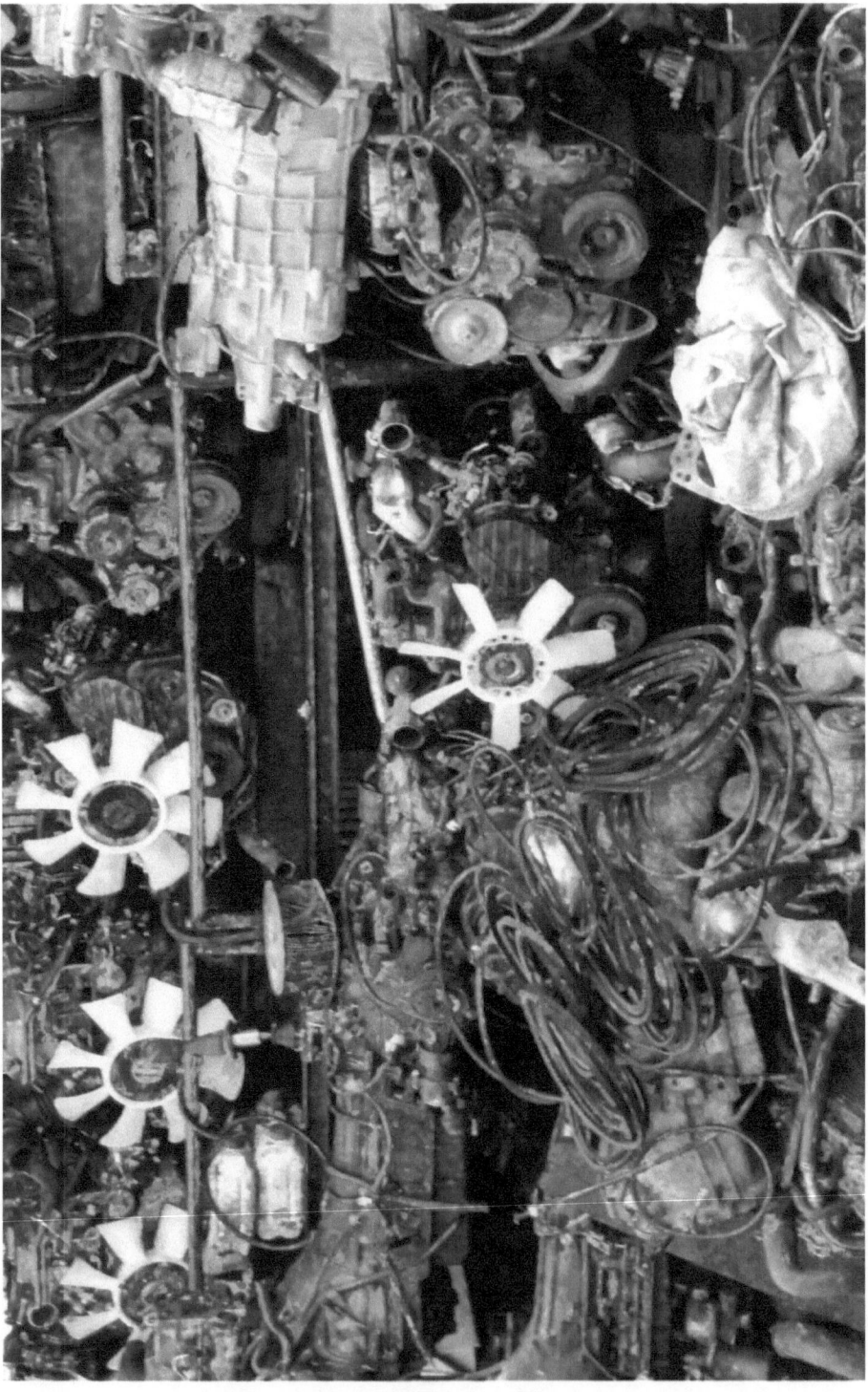

Is There An Electronic Conspiracy Against Me?

I must get through to that number.
Urgent, desperate, emergency,
But tones sound,
And the tech universe doesn't care.

I treat the computer like a twenty terabyte whore,
Shoving plug-ins up its sweet mother board.
Is a print-out too much to ask for?
Apparently, it is.

The video won't play the picture,
Just snow and static tinsel.
It doesn't matter though,
Since in the world of my TV,
The blue is red and the red is green,
And plays only one channel.

The CD skips,

Like scratch-plagued rounded vinyl.

The radio picks up signals from other dimensions,

That noise certainly isn't from this planet.

The microwave keeps ice tray water hard.

As I eat black charcoal from the toaster,

The fridge accidentally warms my dinner too soon.

I walk for my car,

Sleep late for my alarm clock.

The burglar alarm donates my possessions

to non-charitable bodies.

An amuck hairdryer causes baldness,

My electric toothbrush begets me dentures.

But I can't complain-

Because the telephone's broken.

Time to simplify and
the mechanical automaton
computes.

Time to love the simple
things, shallower than the
cosmos, simpler than life,
simpler than death.

Just my knee...

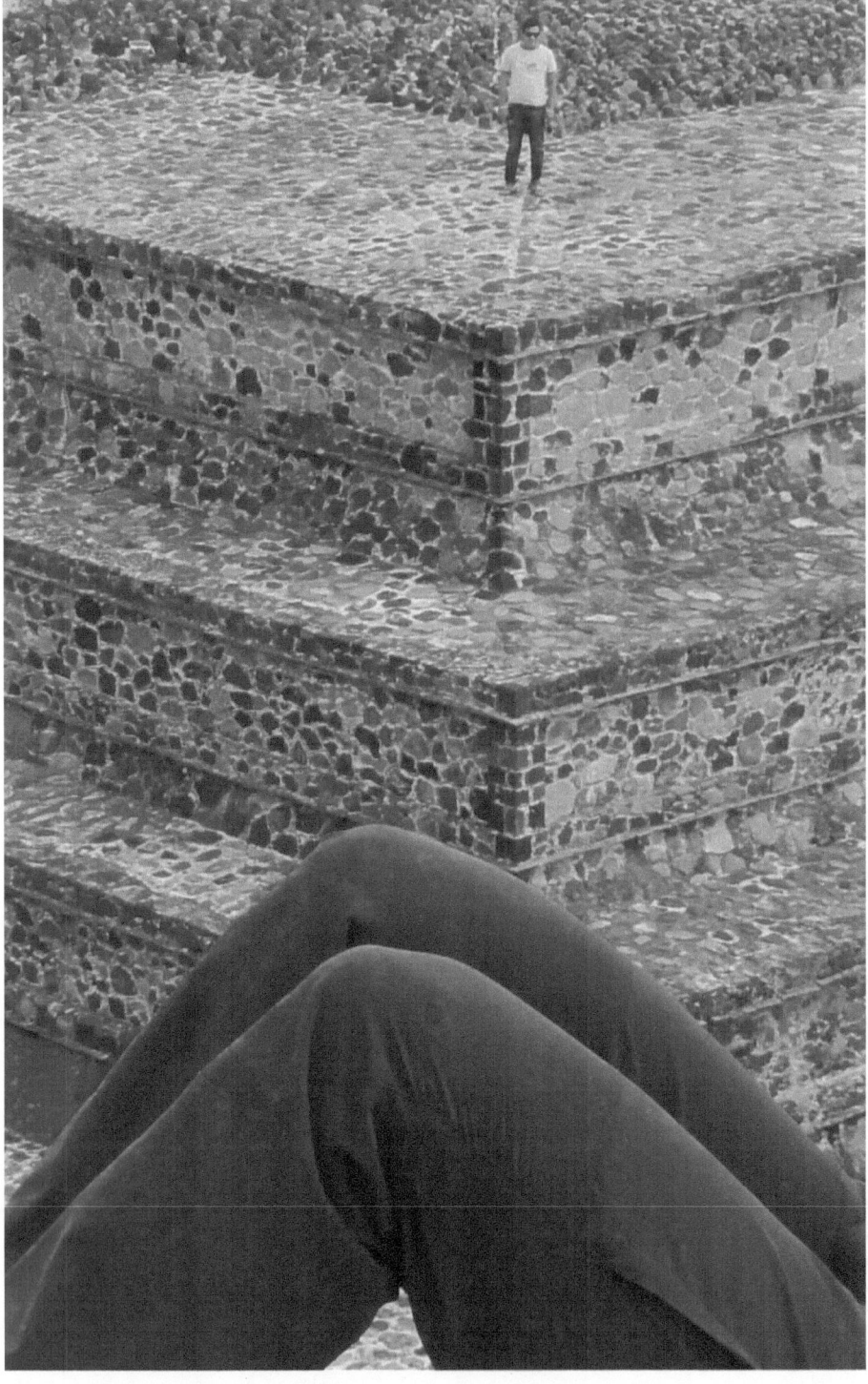

I LOVE MY KNEE

The flowers are bright,
Tis something to see.
From morn to midnight,
I love my knee.

My shoes are tight,
Oh Christ they ache me.
But I've seen the light,
I love my knee.

My frozen mouth scowls,
Doesn't mean to be.
Now I've aching bowels,
But I love my knee.

Too much love of simple complicates, too much contentment breeds internal war.

The fight ahead...

in the house of phantoms, the building devoured people. It feasted on desperate naive souls.

It was a battle for my life.

It was the battle OF my life.

There was **nothing to gain** but my life.

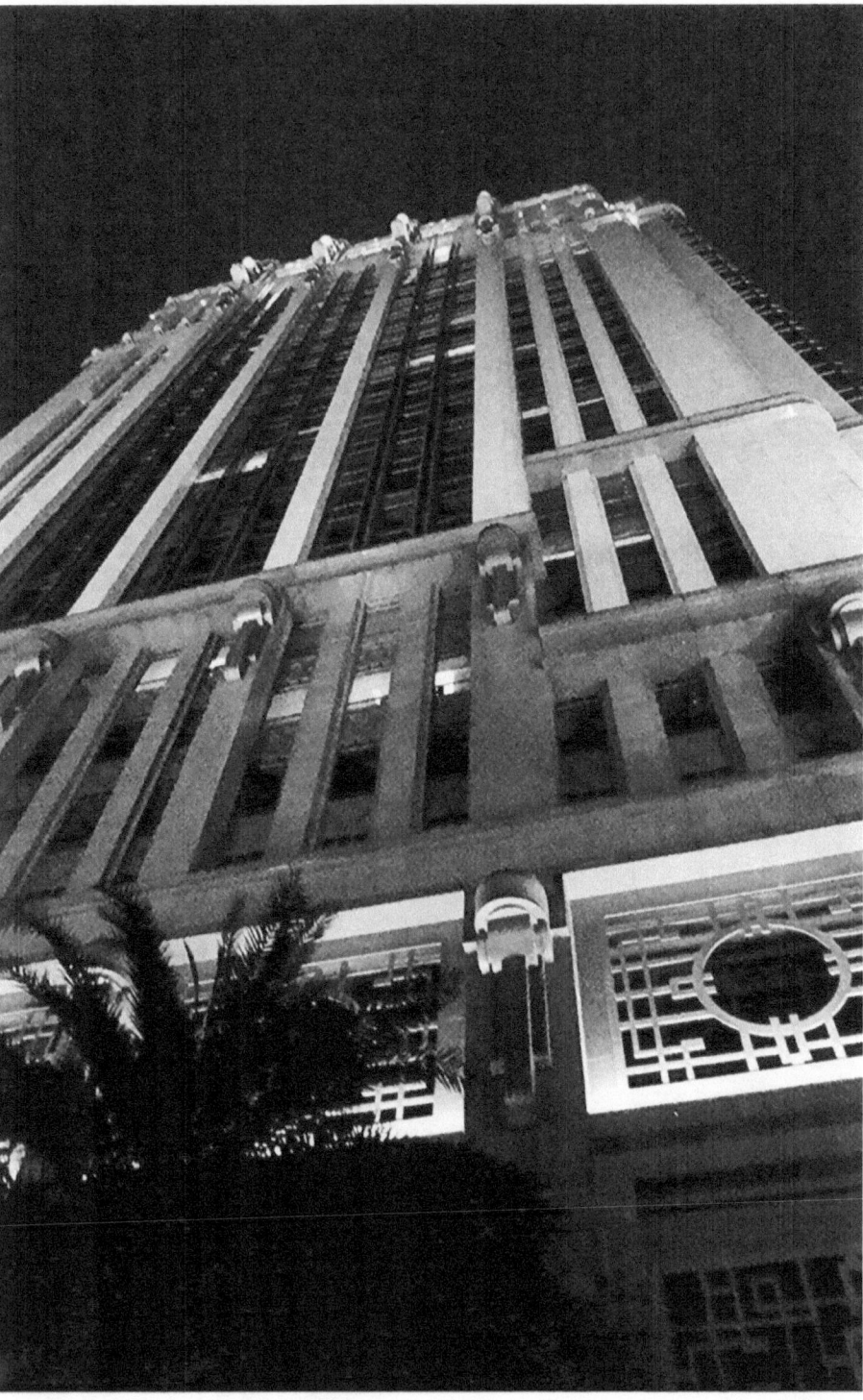

THE BUILDING

In still depths of the unholy building,
Lay a creature awaiting a fight.
Lurk the unknown seeking its victim,
Stalks a parasite bleeding the night.

It waits for me round every corner,
It camouflages itself in the red.
It forces my strongest obsession,
No surrender till either lay dead.

To return to it bravely for battle,
Not to yield to its unearthly moan.
To do battle with a being that is stronger,
To fight and defeat evil's unknown.

I lost the battle but don't suffer,
As I lay painfully gasping for air.
Only you my friend know of my battle,
No-one else is alive to care.

So take heed dear friend of my warning,
Don't enter this building at night.
It's the time when its forces are strongest,
For a mortal to win the unholy fight.

There was just a fool waiting to die, waiting to see if there was an afterlife, or after the afterlife, or anything.

As much as I longed for home, I am to stay here in this skin dungeon.

I am the fool.

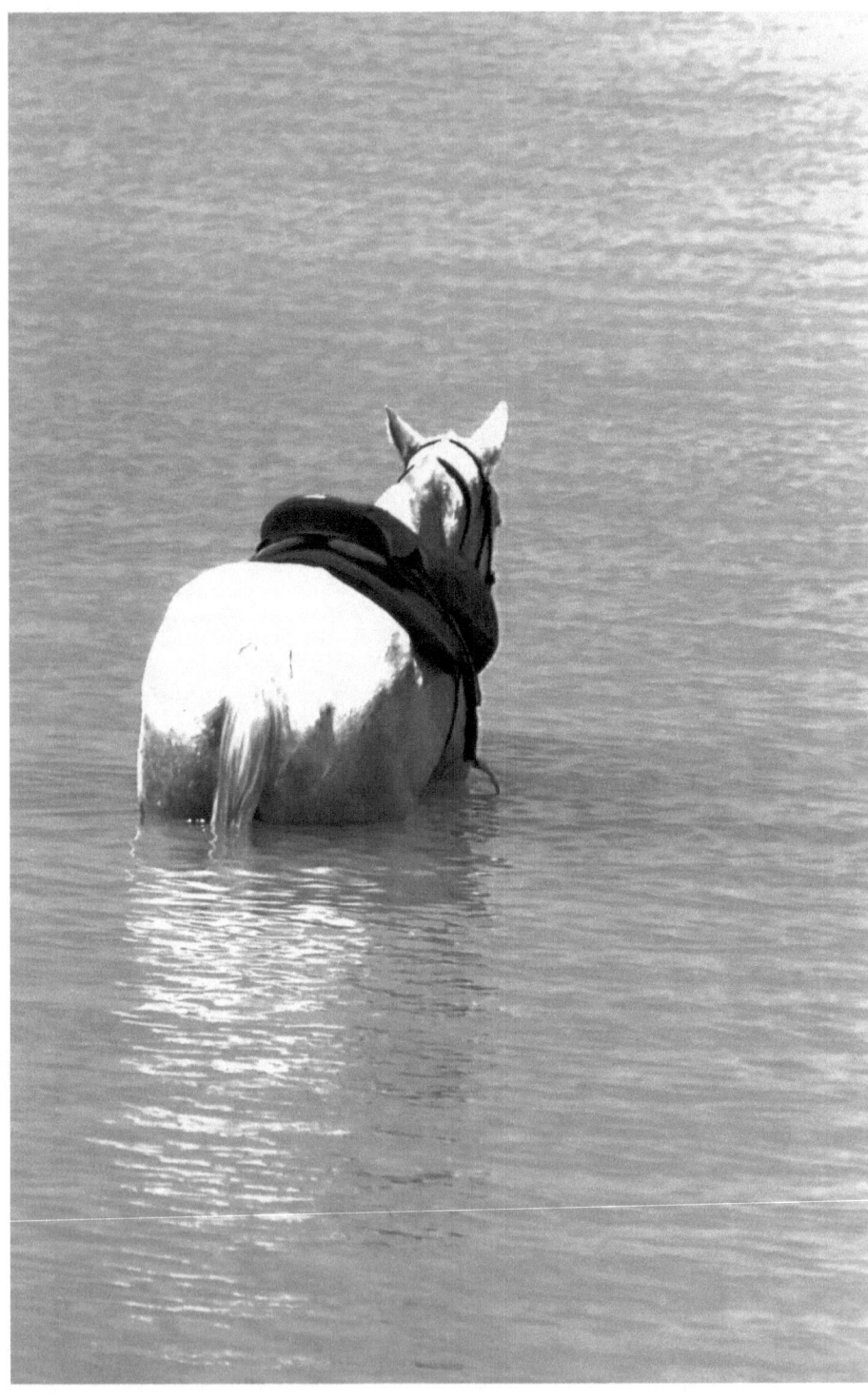

The Fool

The way to see life,
Is to play the fool.
By strolling past strife,
You attend nature's school.

Everyone needs something of me,
But no one demands of the fool.
Everyone charges their fee,
But no one admires the jewel.

There aren't enough fools on the shelf,
For God's-sake we need more.
I want to be a fool myself,
So I can stop keeping score.

There's no happiness alone,
I often feel very sad.
I was once a fool in love,
And now I'm a foolish cad.

Nowhere to hide,
Nobody ever gives.
If a fool commits suicide,
A businessman lives.

And there was my life:
a legend in my own mind, a
genius in my own mirrored
eyes, viewed through such a
narrow perspective.

I wasnt the fool.

The fool is the wisest and
most aware of all.

The fool sees the folly
and that authenticity
elevates him.

My penalty for being a
poor blind fool was to lose
the dearest, most precious,
person in life.

And to live so far from
that person, in distance and
in soul.

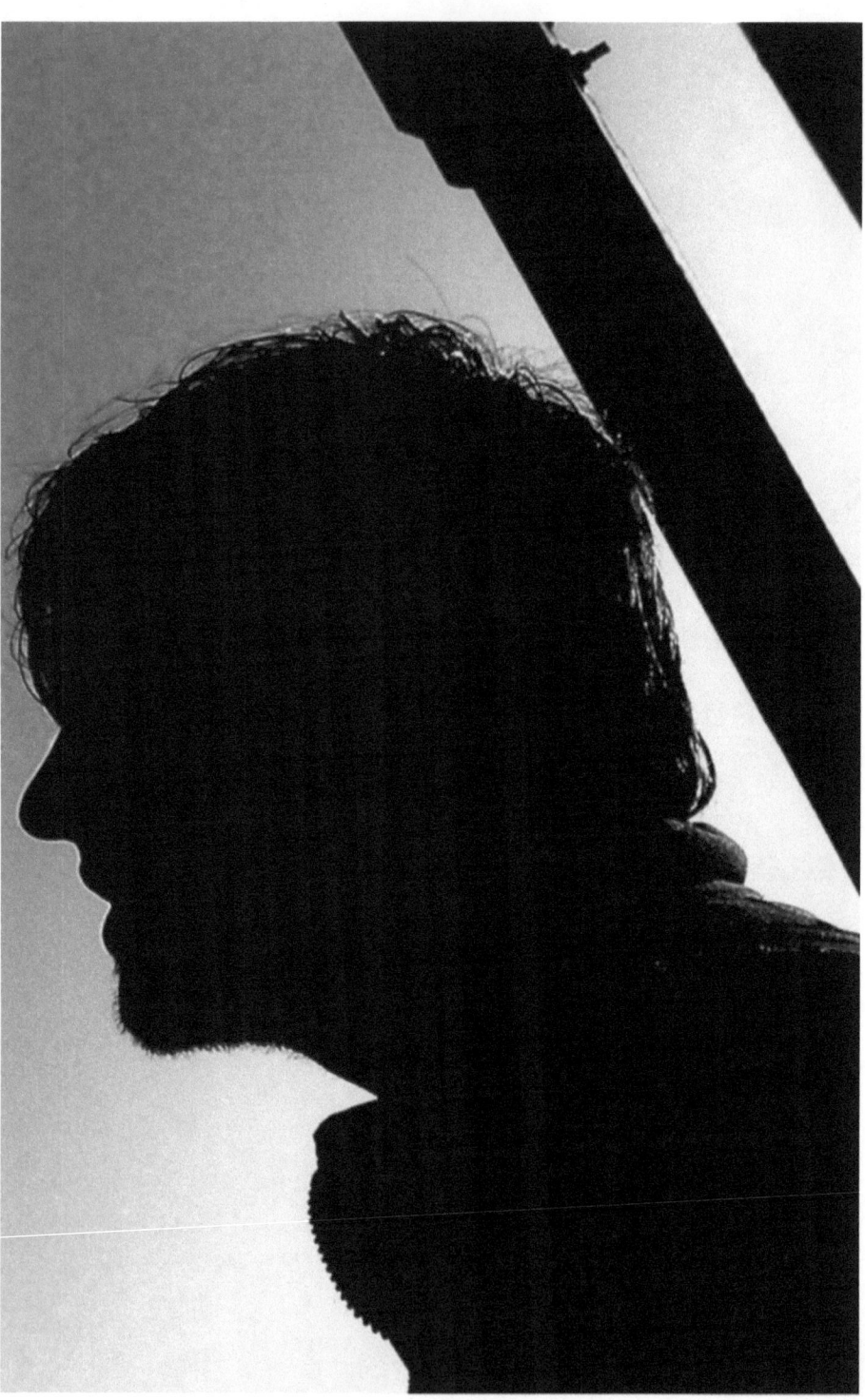

To The Estranged But Never-to-be Forgotten

Such regret I feel in my heart.
Forever, I am wondering,
Who did I need to be?
Who did you want me to be,
That I was blind to?

There is sorrow.
I am sorry.

Who was I,
That I failed you so?
What were my faults,
That I just could not see?
That you could not be with?

I live in sorrow.
I am sorry.

How human should I not have been?
Or how human should I have been?
To lose you,
To never be with that part of me,
That is you.

Unbearable sorrow.
I am sorry.

Is there anything I can do,
To live away your disappointment in me?
Or regret and anger that you feel toward me?
I'm sorry I never was that person you deserved,
I regret being insufficient in being the only one you had.

For that... there is only sorrow.
I am sorry.

There is only the begging,
That you live a rich life.
Happy, fulfilled.
And you never suffer the foolishness,
That I apparently did.
May you never have the pain in your heart,
That I feel.

Such sorrow.
Sorry.

Elliott Stein

I needed to train and
continue to be the best fool
possible.

I plugged my soul
into the flat screen box,
surrendered my mind to the
dim light of the modern
catheter tube dinosaur
re-runs.

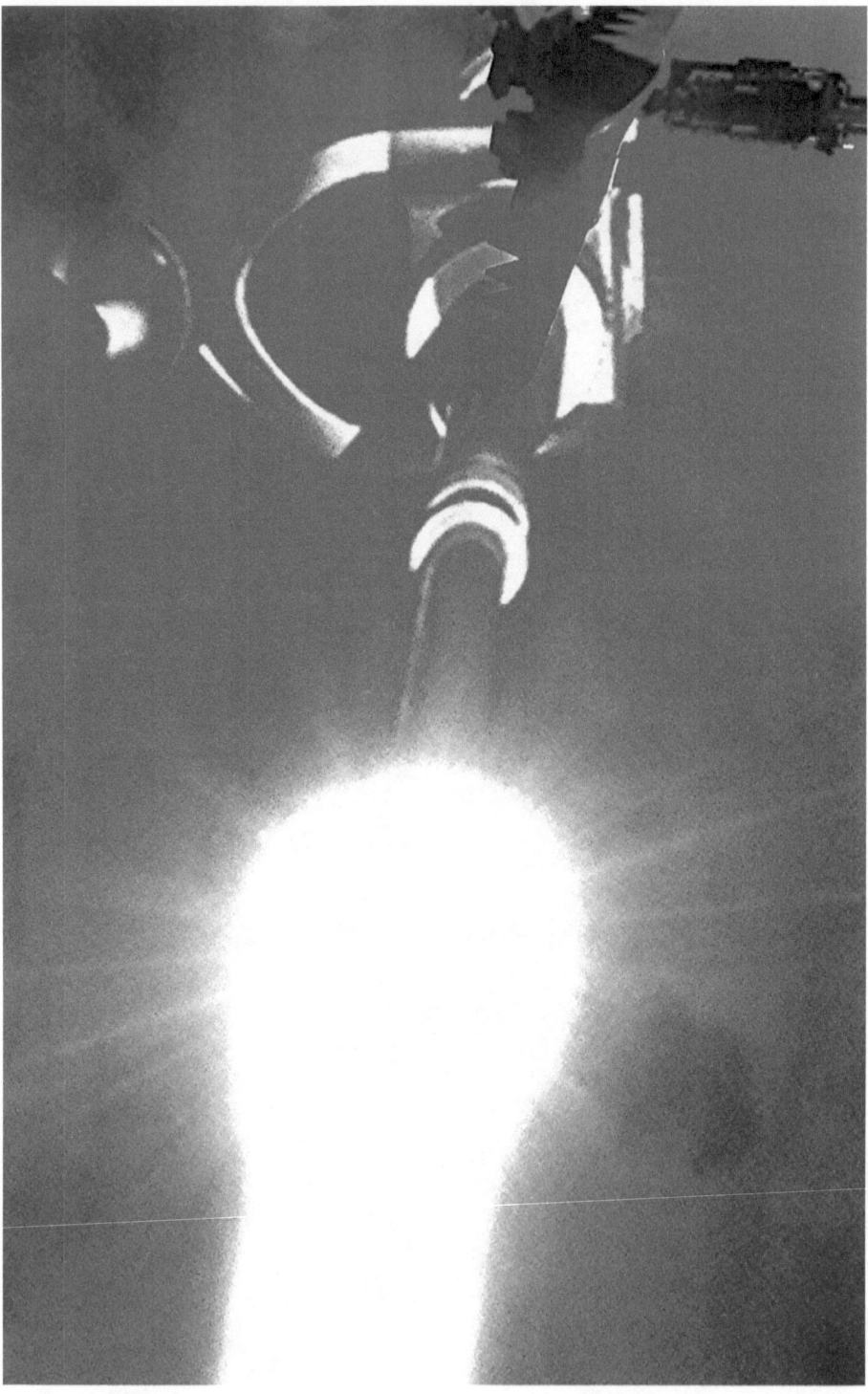

Media Chapter Two

You're my world,
You're my vision,
You're my television.
You're the speaker in my ears,
The picture before my eyes,
What-ever dress, Which-ever disguise.

You're my screen of life,
My speaker of truth.
My flat screen 3d wife,
You're the o'mighty heroic sleuth.

For my drama, for my action,
By the horror of my reaction.
For the good guys and the bad,
The joyous times and the sad.

You're my world, you're my vision,
You're my television.
You're my world, you're my vision,
You're my television.
You're my world, you're my vision,
You're my television.

I - AM – YOU !

I dont just consume, I feed
the monster.

Selling out is so easy
when youre numb, when youre
resigned, when youre a
writing whore.

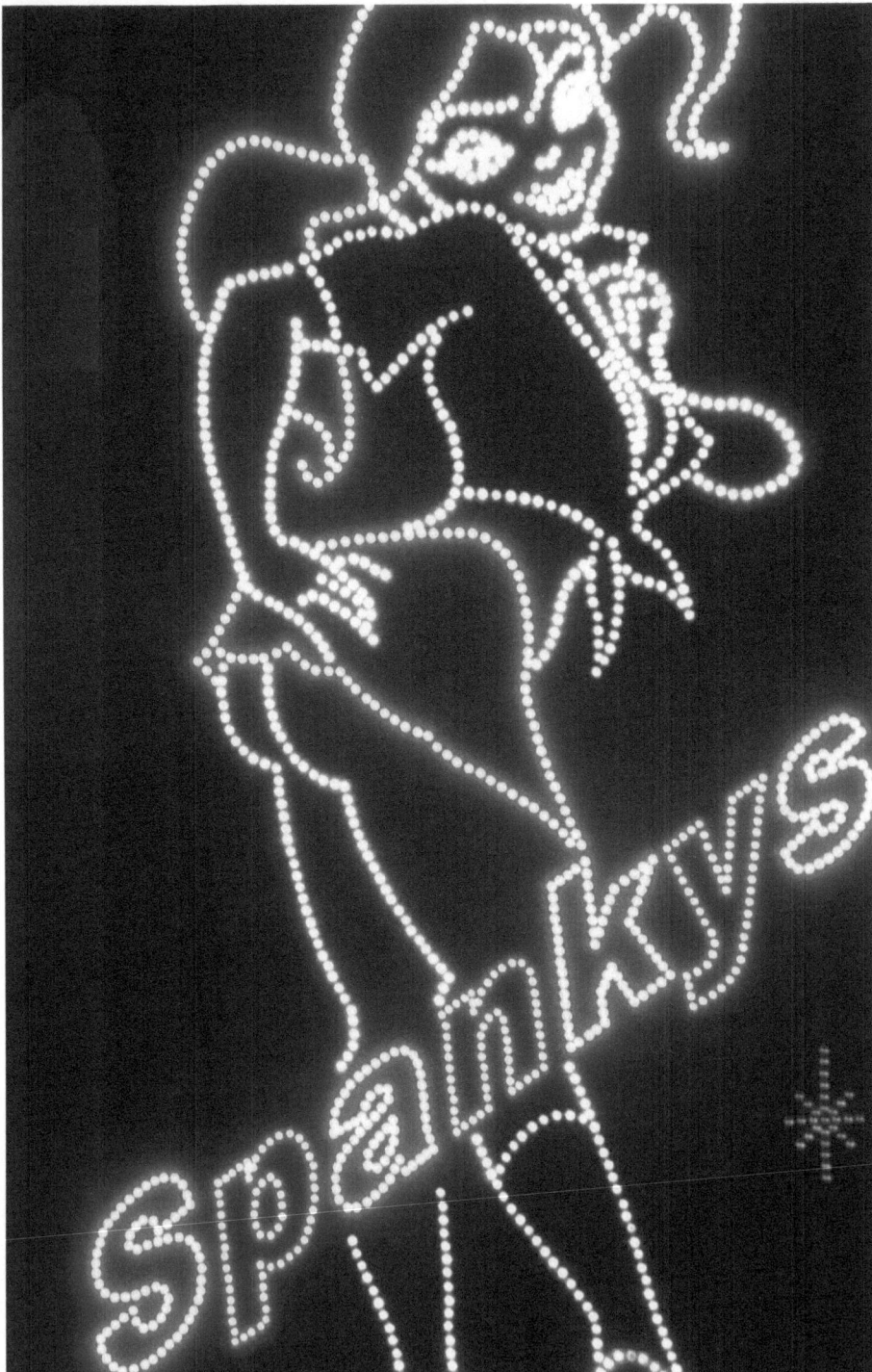

Writing Whore

I'll kiss your ass for money,
No self-respect is in my way.
I'll scare you or make it funny,
I'll dredge whatever for my pay.

I'm a writing whore,
A predictable clichéd breed.
A pontificating scribing bore,
I'll scribble what you need.

I'll give you anything but heart,
Plod tired formats to the letter.
Pay my advance before I start,
For my fee you won't get better.

I'm such a writing whore,
I rip off stories left and right.
I don't have to think anymore,
I just dance around copyright.

My style wreaks of sleaze,
The characters two dimensions thick.
The plot's thinly sliced cheese,
And I know every tired trick.

I'm your private writing whore,
Talent is all I lack.
Work's become a worn-out chore,
I'm your tin-eared pimped-out hack.

Dumbed-down and not too smart,
It fills in the empty space.
It's all product never art,
Thank God I have no face.

I'm a soulless writing whore,
A plotting formulaic tease.
The bar's touching the floor,
I just fuck these computer keys.

While watching my
television, and eating their
little TV dinners, oh rot the
ordinary man and woman and
inbetween.

The pale waffle of their
polite dinner conversation
countered the social
niceties, social graces, and
emptyheadedness.

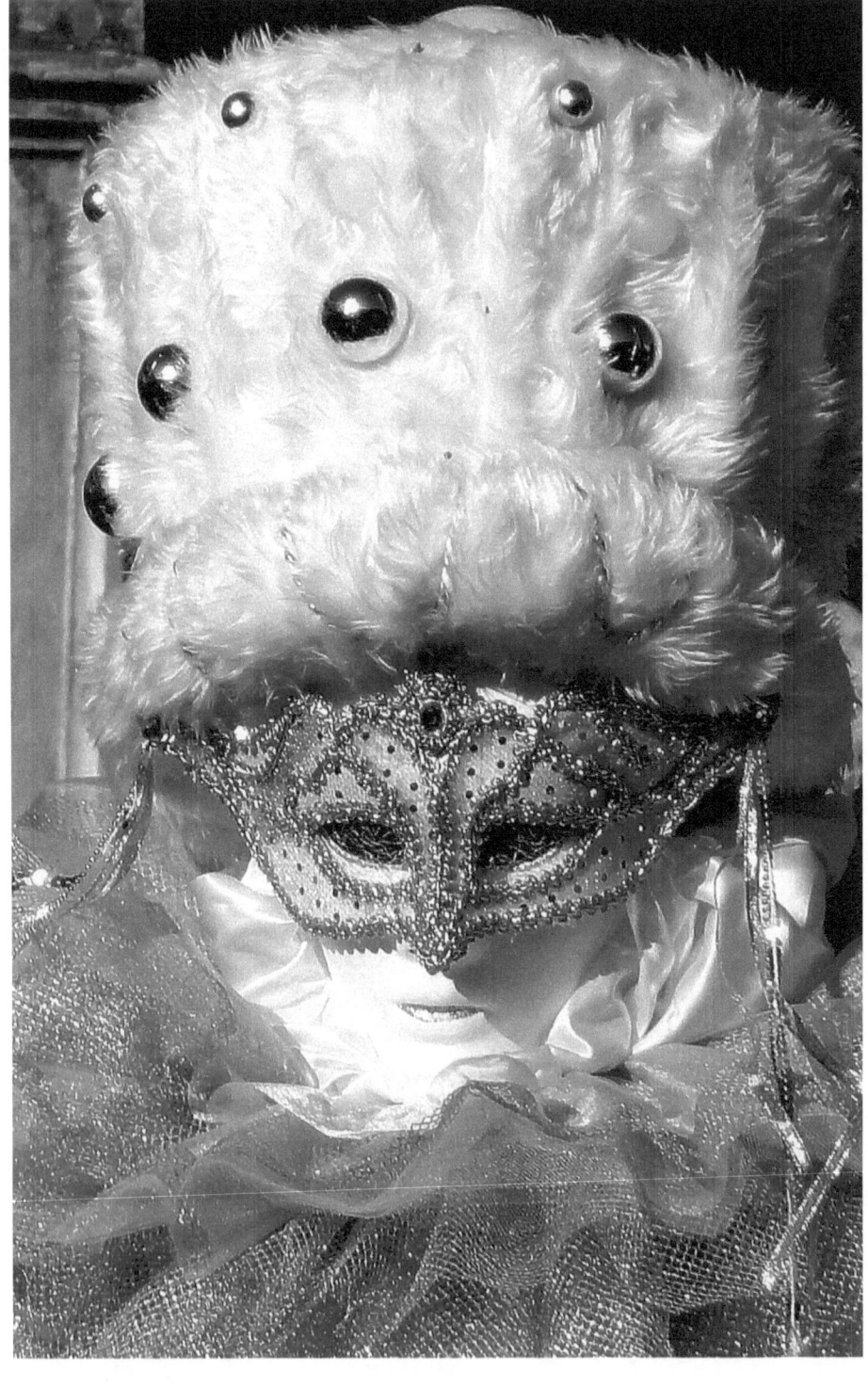

Ode To Empty Headed

Open your mouth and say nothing,
You talk so much about nothing.
You know so much about nothing,
You've never said a meaningful thing.

Politics, sports or the weather,
Or someone's painful gall stone.
It sounds like a record on backward,
When you open your flap to your phone.

Ignorance must be bliss,
Or else you'd be frowning all day.
You always seem to be rather happy,
When talking my life away.

Try to think before you open,
Try to think of what you can say.
I'd rather you listen to me,
But you'll keep talking anyway.

Thank you idiot box, my
head is now conditioned.

I had believed everything
that was told to me by my not
quite elected government.

If they are in power it
must be true.

I listened to their story
of the towers and believed
every lie as the lie was less
scary than the truth.

The lie is hell disguised.

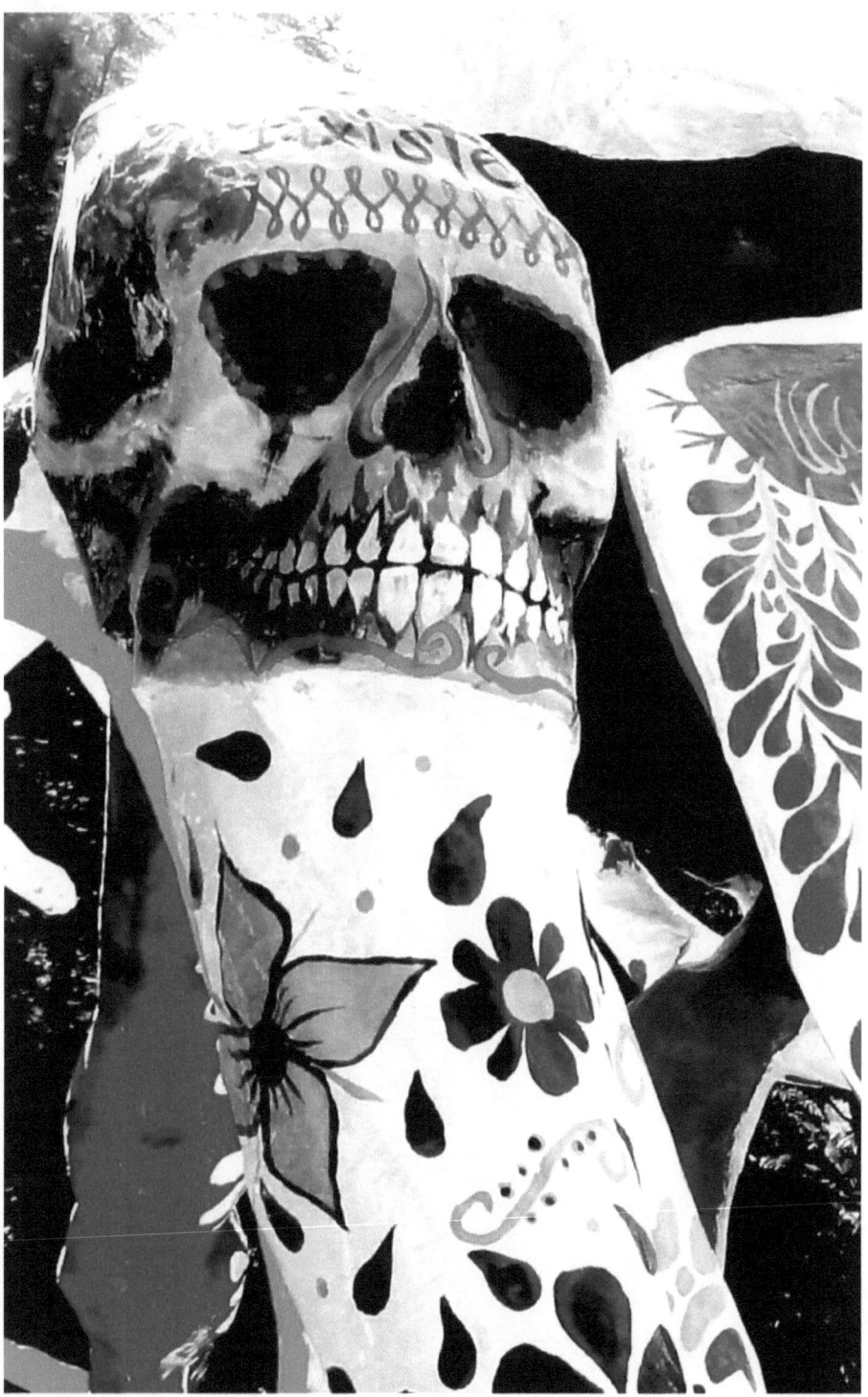

Don't Be Afraid
To Go To Hell

Don't be afraid to go to hell,
No matter what they say.
'Cause I know it well,
I live there everyday.

You're not a stranger,
You live in hell with me.
You know the danger,
It's everything you see.

Live through hell with me,
Together we'll conquer the dark side.
Burn in hell and see,
This time we won't hide.

Defiant of death,
In every breath.
The greatest sin,
Is nobody can win.

So dance through hell with me,
Without a care.
Let your tortures be,
If you dare.

Just can't trust that devil man,
He's the typical guy next to you.
And you're his biggest fan,
You deserve all that you're due.

You never fell,
You were always in hell.

The truth is painful,
it induces a rare condition
called thinking.

Dont make me have real
thought, just let me believe
what they tell me to.

I have no problem with
them thinking for me.

Ive booked a holiday of
a lifetime, it is FOR my life
time.

A holiday for idiots.

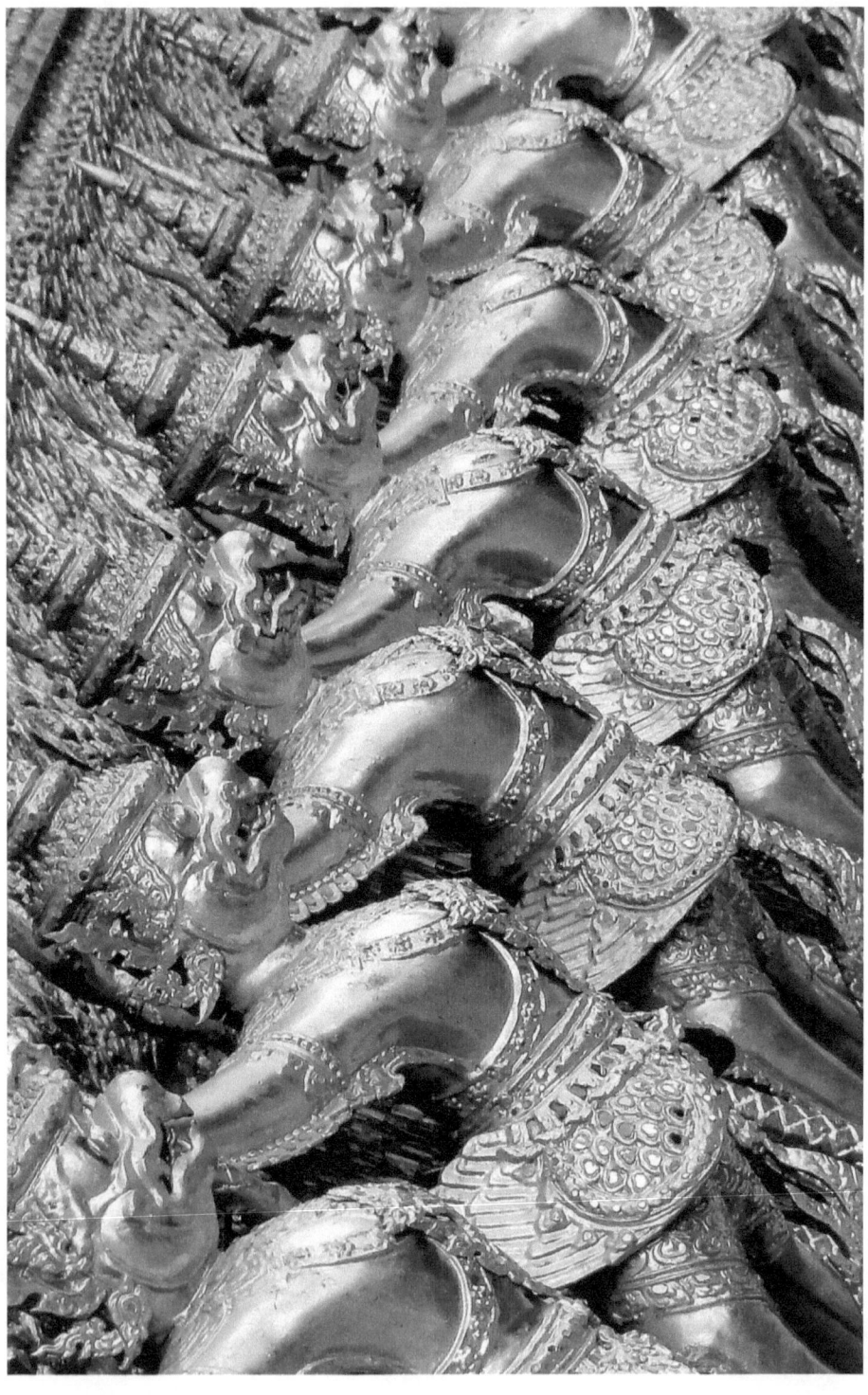

Holiday For Idiots

It's a holiday for an idiot,
Drooling classes held at noon.
A workshop for idiots,
Barking howling at the moon.

Idiots unite and be yourselves,
For the world to laugh and see.
It's a year's holiday for an idiot,
And that suntanned fool is me.

It still wasnt the way I dreamed of it, I was living the wrong fantasy.

It wasnt a life even close to what I wanted, I never wanted to be so much like me.

What I thought the future would be went so misguidedly wrong.

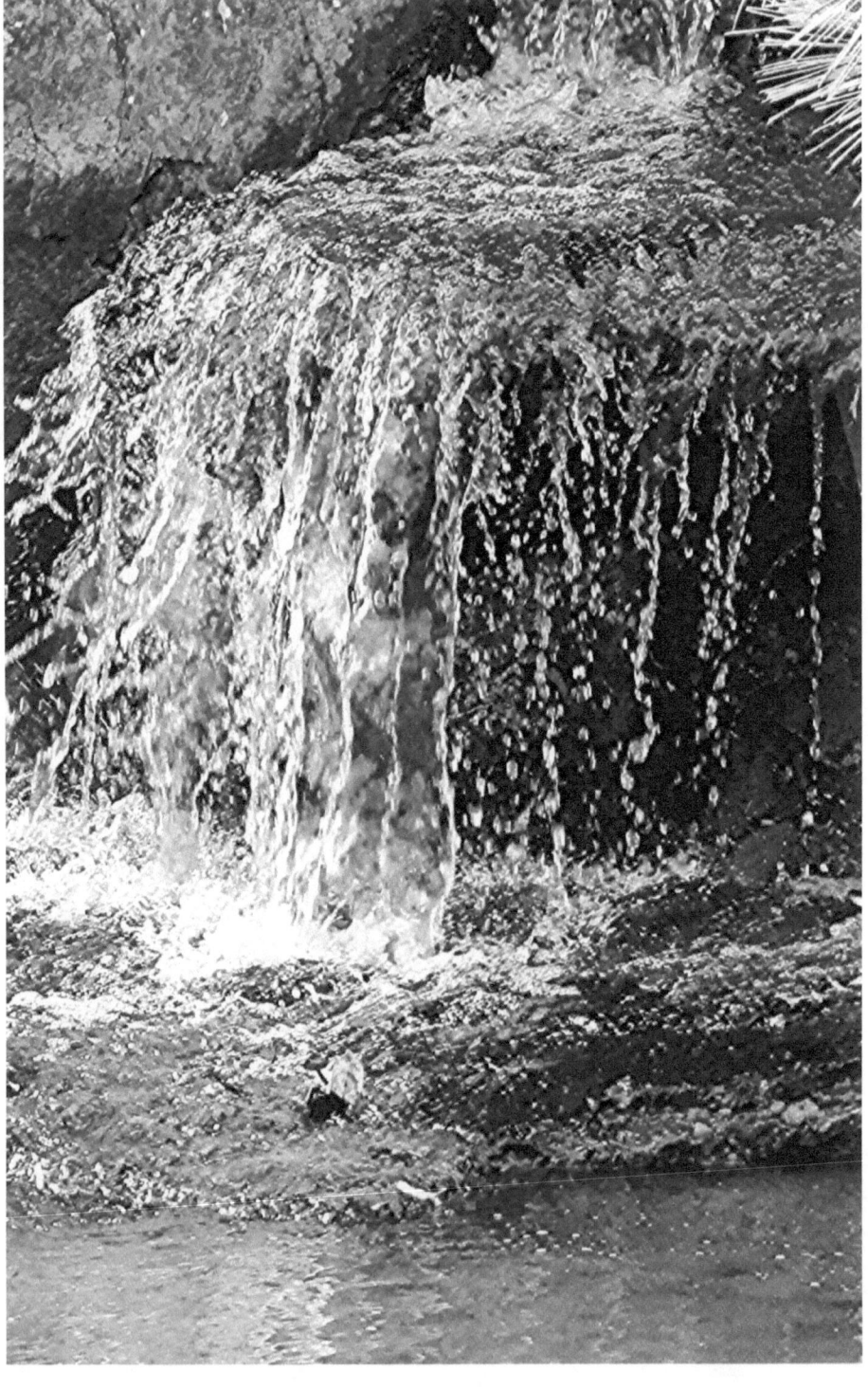

Lifetime Work: Condensed And Combined

(Don't Let The Rain Go Bye)

This isn't the life I created,
I'm living the wrong fantasy.
Never dreamt I'd be so hated,
I never wanted to be... me.

My existence now deleted,
I was born to be abused.
I didn't live to be cheated,
I was created to be used.

Non-existent middle ground,
I never could be found.
A joker said do or die,
Don't let the rain go bye.

Disembodied bodies without faces,
Empty eyes without souls.
Running circular endless races,
Achieving non-existent goals.

Performing on the final stage,
I begged help from the band.
They wrote the final page,
While they cut me off my hand.

To win futile battles in my time,
I am guilty of yesterday's crime.
I was and lived the biggest lie,
God-sake - Don't let the rain go bye.

Today's downright dismal,
Tomorrow looks bleak.
Next day is abysmal,
That continues next week.

Grabbing shadows in the moonlight,
In love with phantoms through the day.
I must be God because I'm always right,
I'm dead as I know what to say.

Elliott Stein

Tomorrow I will live today,
Whilst searching for another way.
No one yet discovered why,
Please don't let the rain go bye.

Falling in love without feeling,
Imagining with and without thought.
I'm never sick but always healing,
Fighting wars I've always fought.

Time dies in my head,
Could it possibly be real?
Am I finally dead?
I must be - I can't feel.

Dying in the forbidden zone,
It's a way to become well known.
It's become an art to die,
But don't let the rain go bye.

Elevators are out,
And staircases are in.
He's never had a doubt,
That the good guys will win.

Let the master actor tell his lie,
Have the audience laugh and cry.
If he doesn't he will wilt and die,
Just don't let the rain go bye.

Don't let my mind go dry,
Don't let me suffer and die.
Don't let the sunshine lie,
Don't let the rain go bye.

Elliott Stein

When an idea dies, when concept fades to imaginations dust, where never is created, that is where never comes the day.

When inspiration turns into a memory, where memory turns into memory, the memory disappears as memory and become the real chains that bind.

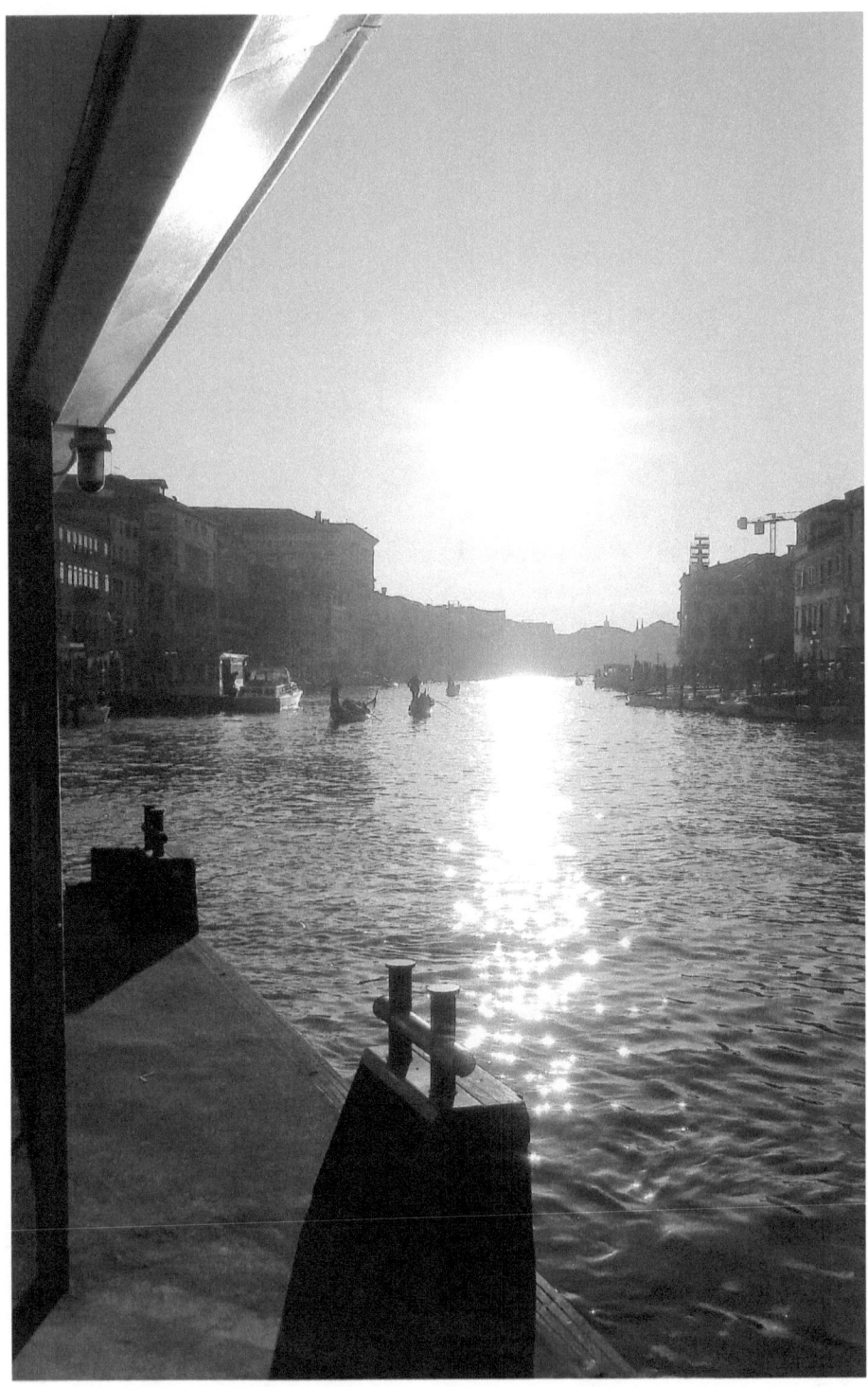

Lifetime Work: Continued And Abused

Beast of the dark,
Lurks through mist.
Sleeping in park,
Clenched hand in fist.

Hawks in moonlight,
Soar majestic and bold.
In the kingdom of night,
Stalks a wolf in the fold.

Red borders the blue,
Near Isle castle light.
Rock leads to history new,
Currents in timeless flight.

On the bridge of stone,
The world finally as one.
In a small rock pond alone,
We die at the evening sun.

Eyes that see,
In realities true.
Far too late for me,
What about for you?

Elliott Stein

I witnessed what came
close to passing for a hero.

Manning looked like one,
his jaw so stereotypically
square.

But that couldnt be seen
in the twilight, where the
night people live or walk
through death.

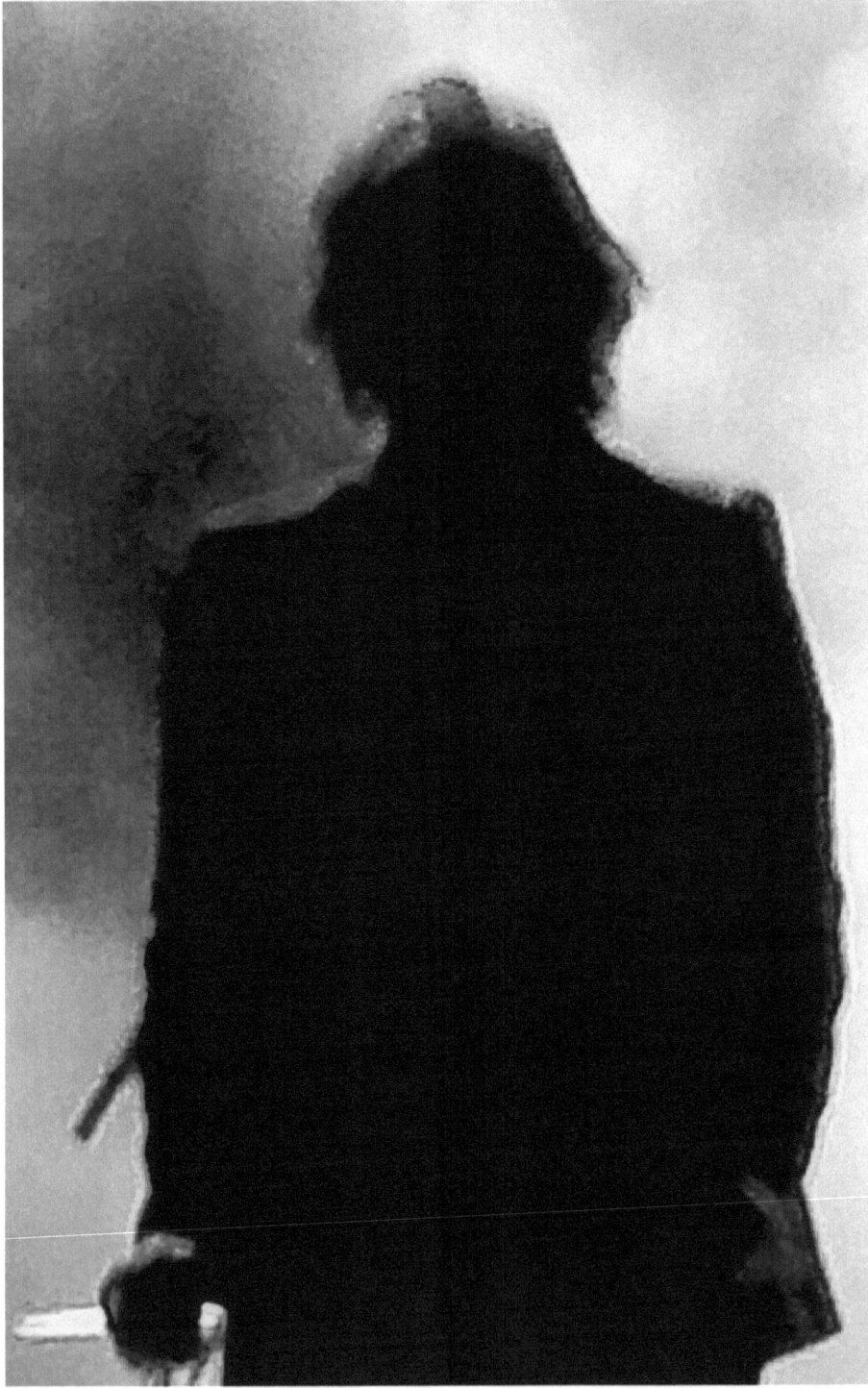

Night People In Twilight Dreams

Manning watches the shadows,
He looks for shapes in the darkness.
He dreams of what's imagined,
He doesn't sleep at night.

He sleeps when he's awake and walking,
He dreams between the heartbeats.
The lapses wander to the next frontier,
Where he lives a different life.

The characters are different,
The stories are alien specter.
When realities don't exist,
There's only that which cries.

Manning is one of the night people,
He screams silently to twilight demons.
They're unleashed from his mind,
They manifest in ether tombs.

Manning is in danger,
He is safe from the fire.
Walk through the graves,
In the field of decay.

Elliott Stein

After the great battles,
whilst lying and waiting
for death to come, even true
believers in something have
nothing.

In different realities of
afterlife, can the nonsensical
be real?

Is heaven and hell as true
as I believe it to be?

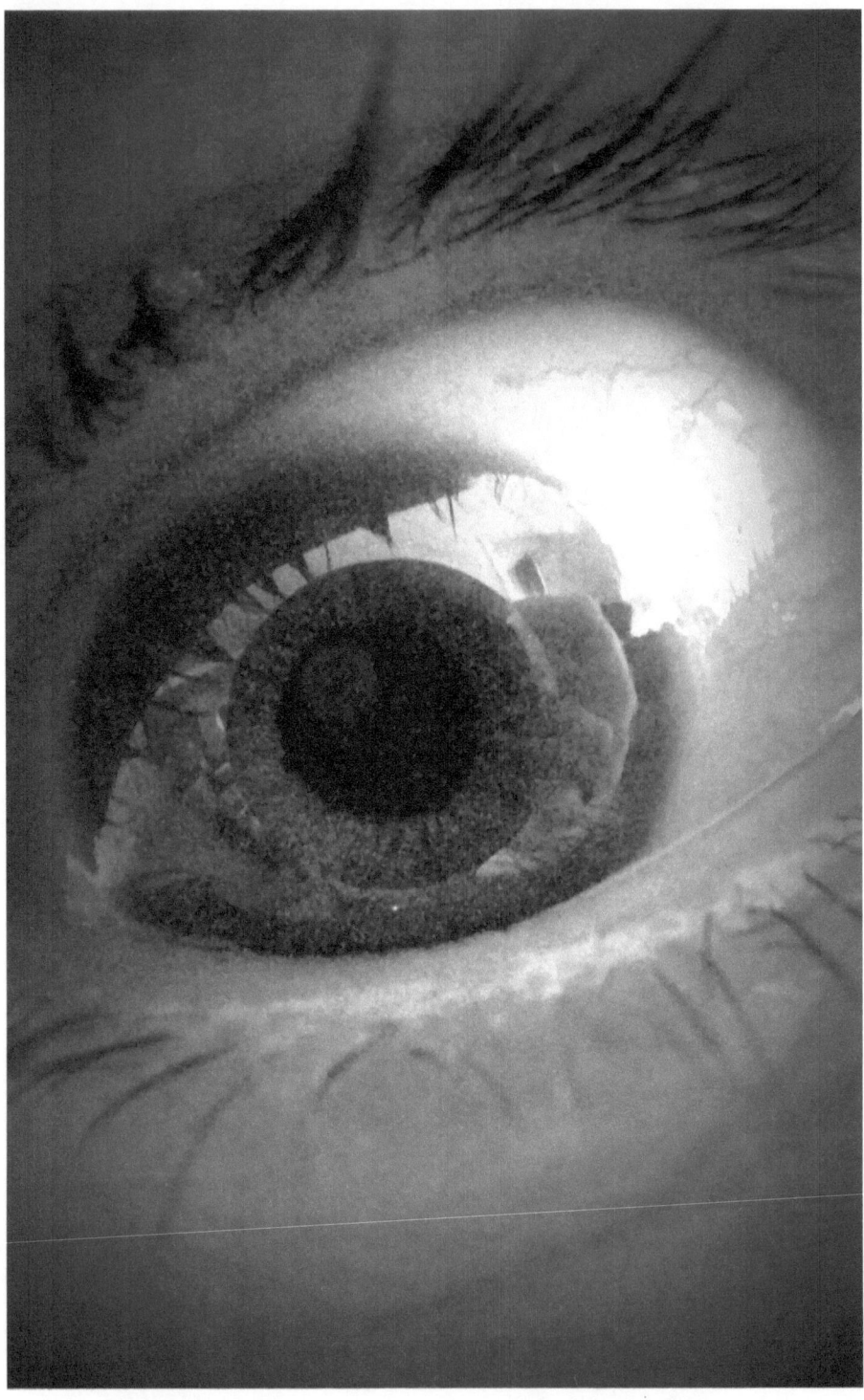

Bleeding Inside

As one like the moon,
Darkness rises soon.
Clouds over my head,
All's finished not said.

There's never a place to hide,
When you're bleeding inside.
There is a type of suicide,
Continue bleeding inside.

Heroes seem smaller,
Tragedies become taller.
Silence echoes silent singing,
Words then lose all meaning.

Mind reaches its height,
Body loses the fight.
Then your eyes begin seeing,
You cease a way of being.

When your crippledness spreads wide,
You start bleeding inside.
When your last love has died,
You are bleeding inside.

Louisiana hookers go on strike and there are no more gators in the hive.

The many afterlife thoughts in my head seamlessly manifest reality.

I see a blemished heaven of soot.

I see unshaven fallen angels, so many broken wings and cracked halos.

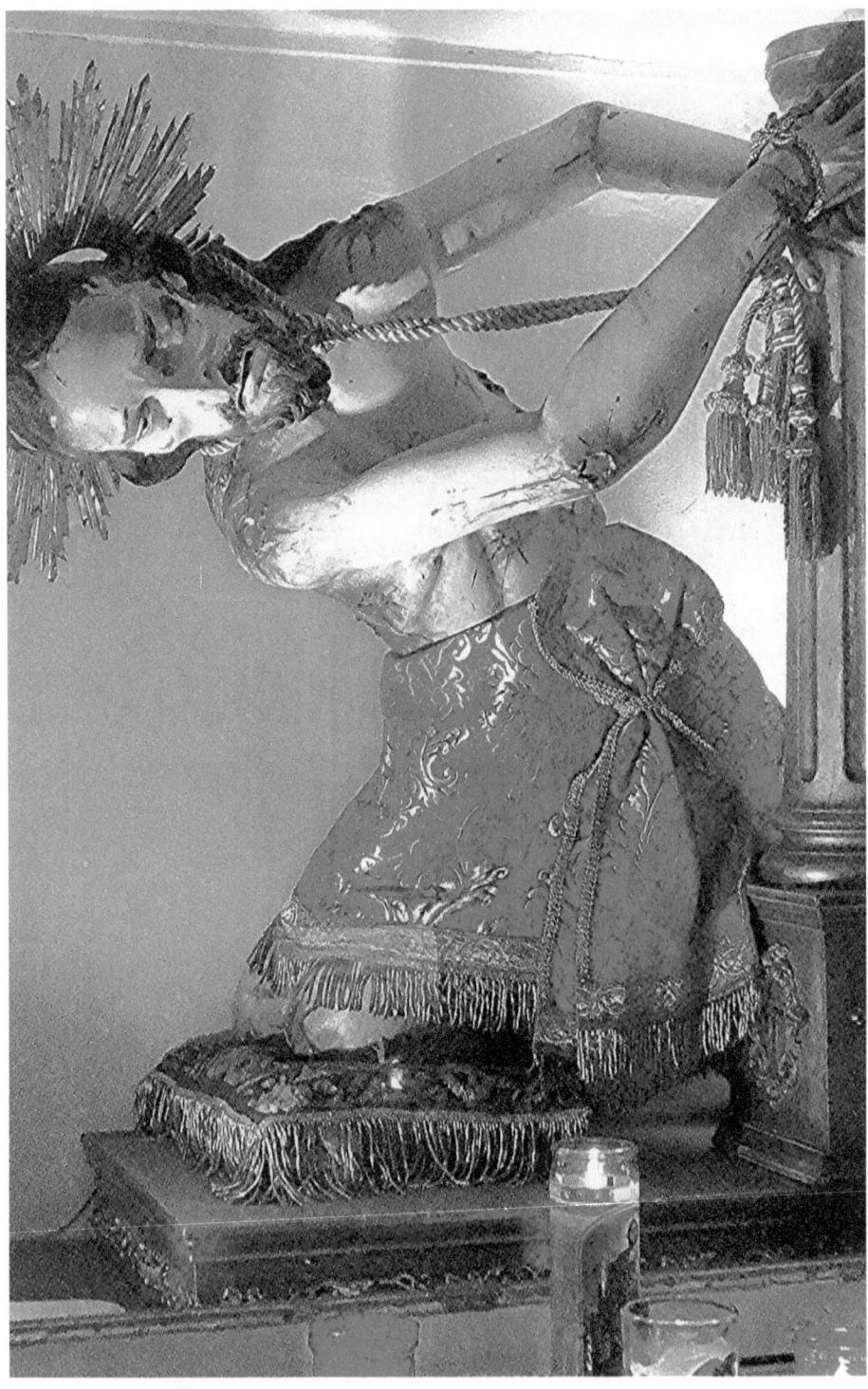

Unshaven Fallen Angels

Slender broken angels,
Beneath the cracked sky.
Tarnished white feathers,
On atrophied wings.

Tears burning to the ground,
Heartbeat in reverse.
Dreams of past visions of defeat,
Eternities of sounds trapped.

Damaged souls decay eternal,
A moment's suffering without end.
Unrelenting running through the tunnel,
The claw crawls across my wrinkled face.

Without forgiveness,
Lacking grace,
Praying for death,
The cruelty won't come.

I saw that the world was experienced through my glaze of dead eyes.

I lived my life in that world, with an illusion of power so separate from what I was and could be.

I performed a post-mortem of my heart.

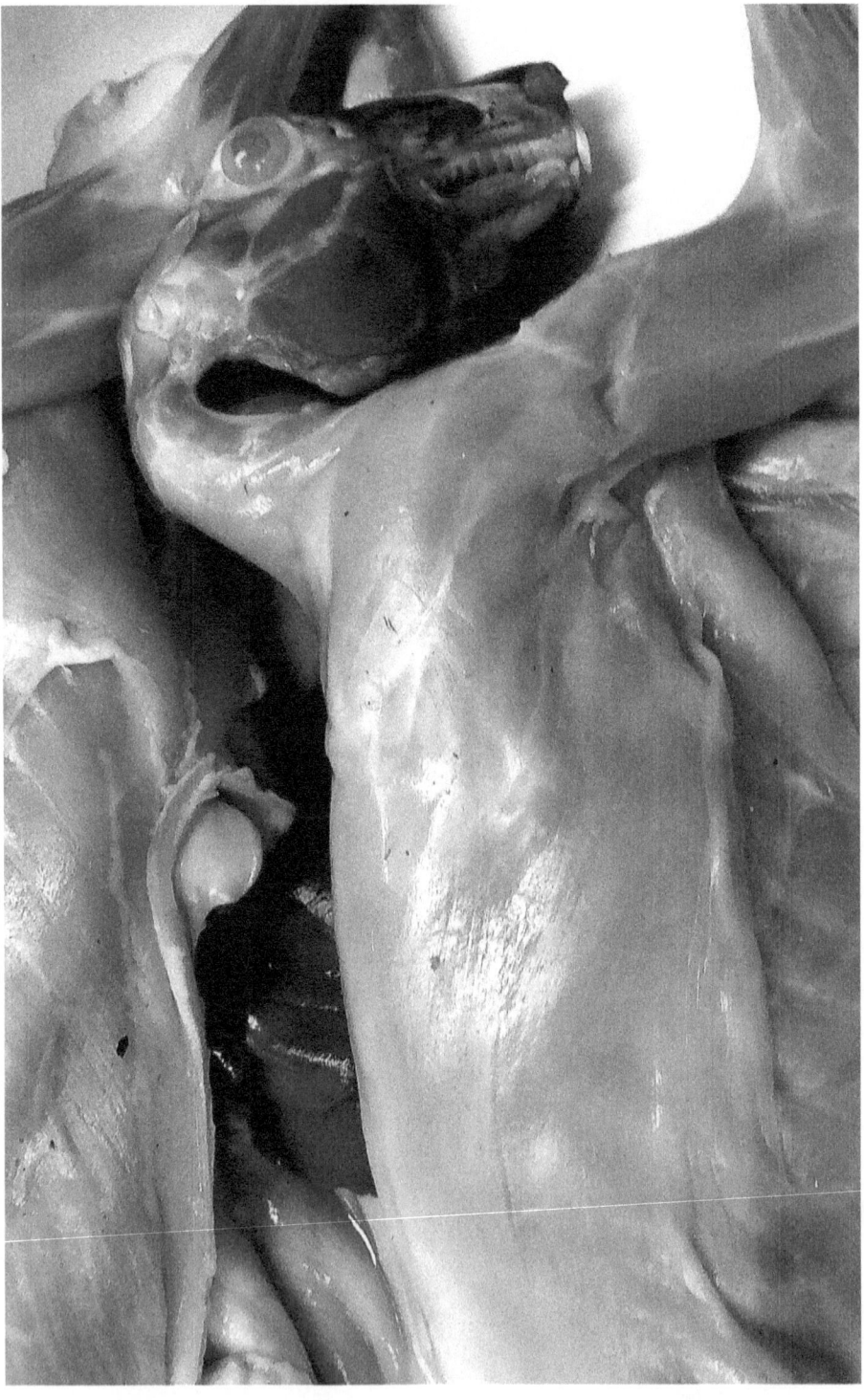

You Know Where Love Has Gone Wrong

As moonlight shatters your dream,
As birds shriek through deadly song.
As nightmares grow blue,
They are all dreams of you,
You know where love has gone wrong.

As the orchestra plays a one note theme,
As souls suffer so deep and so long.
Your open heart is taboo,
So they all dream of you,
That is where our love has gone wrong.

An old beloved friend, I once promised Id love forever, has become a stranger in my heart.

I mourned the marriage I once gave of my soul.

Such a struggle to generate beyond the tide, beyond the air of futility as another relationship comes to end.

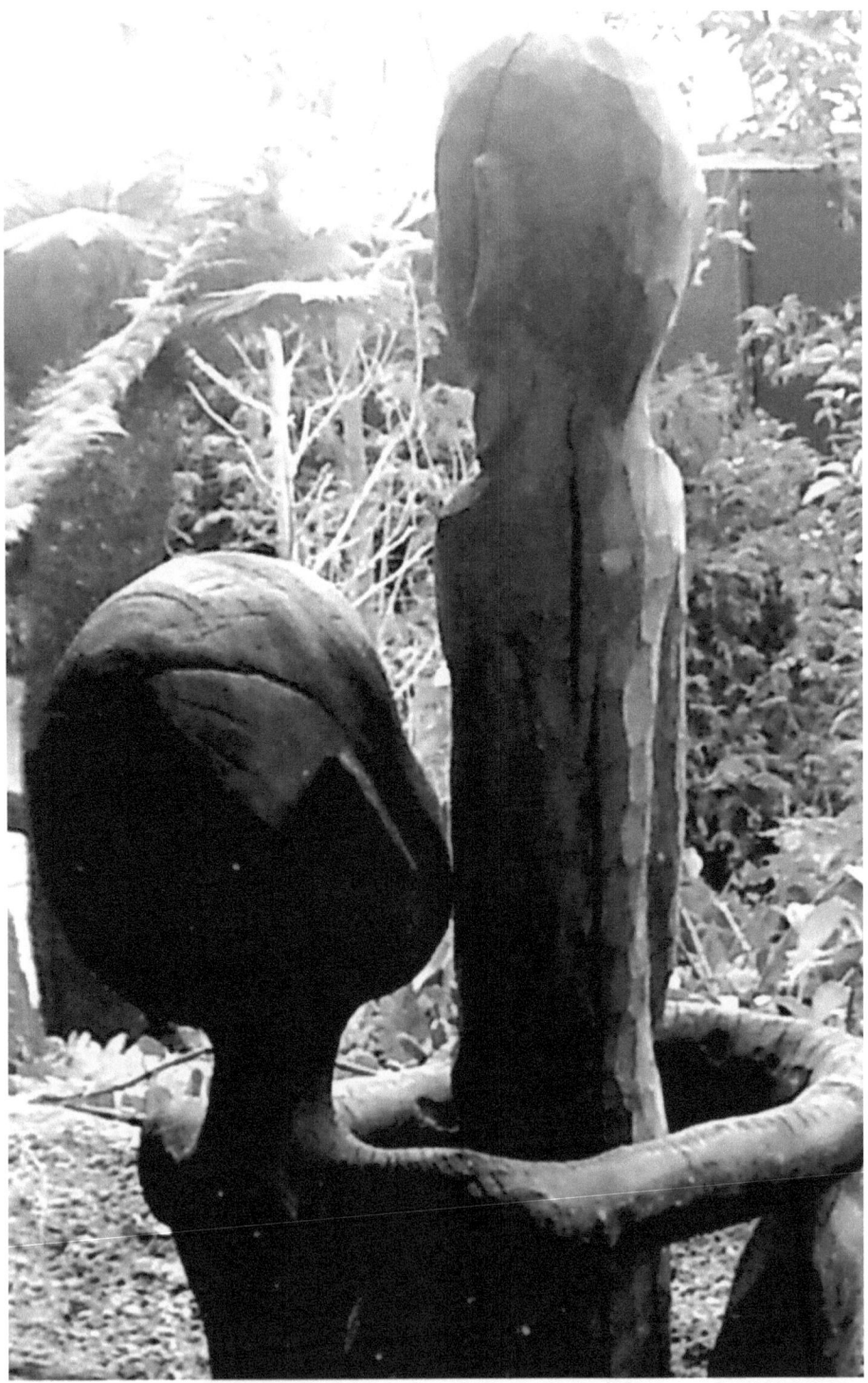

End Of Hearts

Every love seems to end the same,
And begin with naive notations of forever.
Though I envision it coming at the end,
I never believed it could at the beginning.

That feeling it is about to be over,
Distance o' cutting in my heart.
Cannot speak the words I know I should,
Inexorable destinies of separate souls.

The expanse together is deafening,
So lonely in one-another's cold arms.
The dark sadness of the inevitable,
Embracing a loneliness to come.

Knowing where it is to go,
Self-induced blindness to the end.
Painful numbing the pain to be,
Bitterness reaps a soul barren.

More regrets added to the growing burden.

Determined not to cry at heartbreak, I wouldnt let it touch me, I couldnt let it show.

So we will be adult and shrug it off and pretend it doesnt hurt.

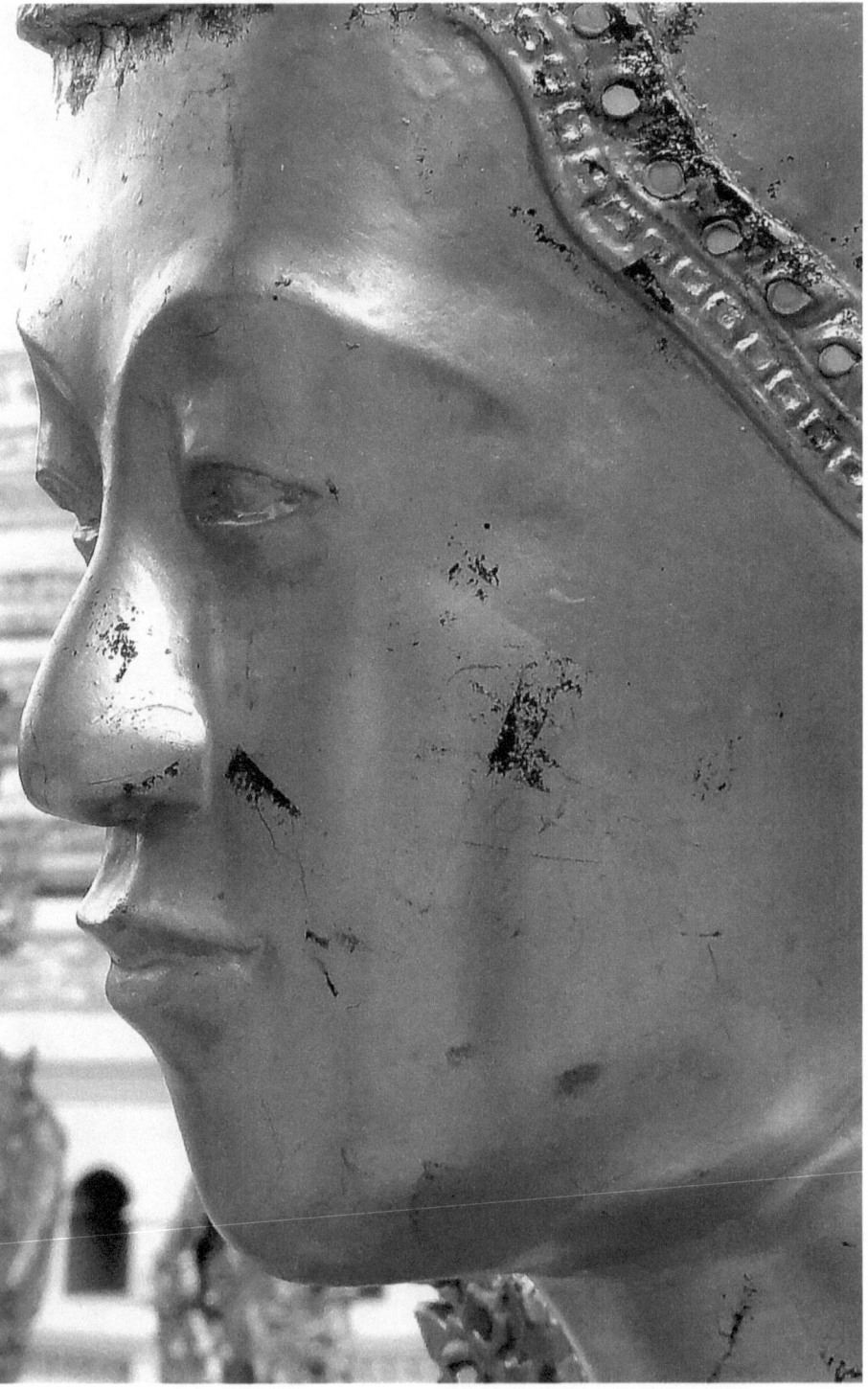

Platitudes Of The Lonely

Goodbye.
I am sorry.
I regret what happened,
It didn't have to be this way.

We could have made it work,
Oh well… nothing lasts forever.
Its best we move on,
Let's be friends.

I need time to get over this,
Let's just see other people.
We'll keep in touch… okay?
We'll divide our things.

How are you getting on with your life?
It wasn't all bad.
It was a learning experience,
Sad it didn't work out.

If only I…,
If you just didn't…,
We could have…,
Goodbye.

Till death do us part was
not our passage to be set free,
till death brings us together
again in lives and death
through eternity.

And as for promising
to love and obey... are you
kidding me?

I wont make the mistake of opening my heart and laying it bare.

I strip all moral pretention from the mix. I dont care about romance.

Lets just get laid and after that... laid again.

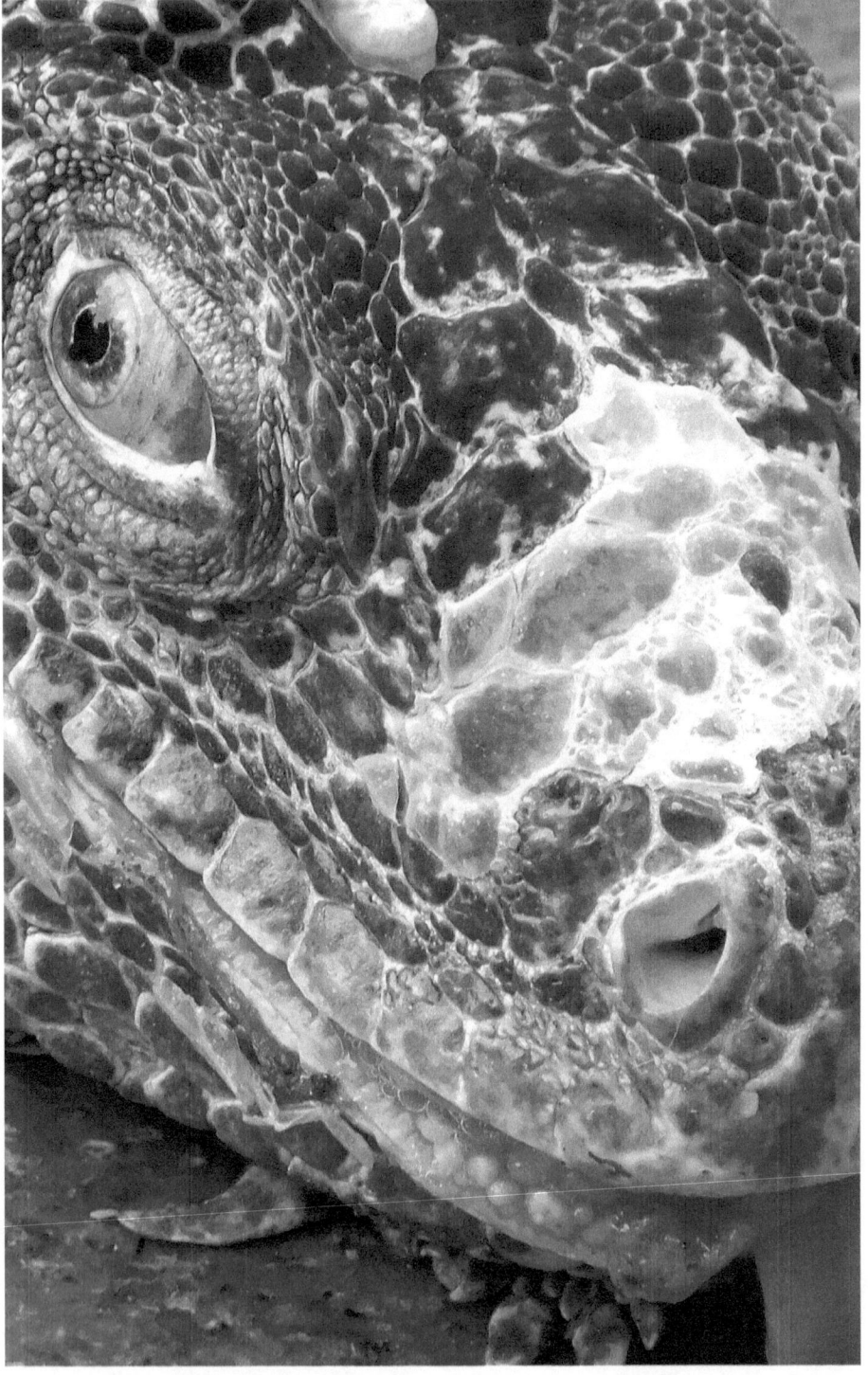

sex on mind

As I pretend higher noble thoughts,

Whilst I impersonate a deep thinker,

All I think about is your clothing removed,

That desert animal's walking apparatus exposed.

And various phallic shaped objects inserted,

In the place I imagine that red taster of mine to be.

As much as I nod my head to your

worthy intellectual arguments,

I am picturing an image of such carnal intimate acts,

That would make even a Catholic bishop blush.

For what he fancies doing with that choirboy,

Is what I fancy doing with you.

My mind's eye possesses x-ray vision,

As you walk toward me I see beneath it all.

The shirt and bra do not hide the fullness of those breasts,

Not even lead undies could shield the erotic delight,

Of your ever delectable secrets that I crave and long for.

And don't ever give your heart to my charms,
Do not ever think of me as respectable,
Though I masquerade under that pretense so well.
All my noble thoughts and gestures,
Are designed with but one purpose in mind:
To be delightfully inside you.

And after I win your heart,
After my ever so sweet victory,
I will coldly move on to the next warm body,
And that prey be my next conquest.

Nothing personal,
It's just what I do.
I'm not going to buy you a mink,
I'm just going for the pink.

Elliott Stein

Heaven proves to be a construct of my own creation.

I think the angels are whole, I imagine the clouds repaired, and so they are.

I also refurbish hell: fire with much more style.

So I sit in a room for three days.

Part of me is up front leading, Im surrounded by more of me whos forgotten.

Im resisting it, but wanting it, and praying it is for real.

It wasnt real. It was more powerful than that.

It made a difference.

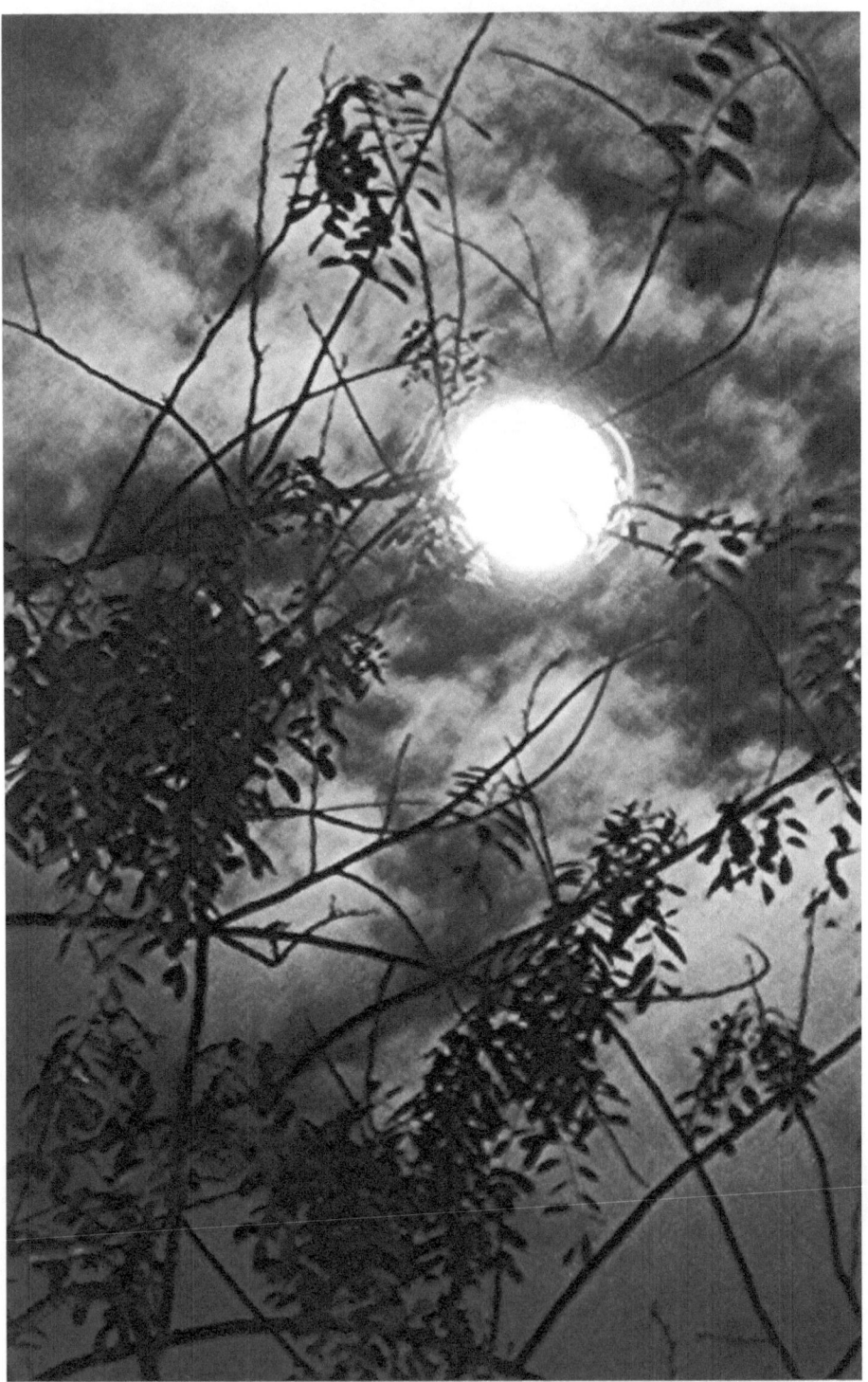

Transformation

Such tragic magic,
Eyes of darkness.
Shades of pure gray,
In the mind of soul.

Where did it all go?
It was never here.
Ended before the start,
Began at the end and decayed.

As hard as I try,
Tis no more life in the box.
It was never here and now gone,
For bloody ever and a day.

It's all make believe,
Farcical shadows of never-to-be.
Nights of madness,
Phantom visions at heart.

Quiet whispers diminish,
The silence forcing its will.
Upon unsuspecting reality,
In collective minds and hearts.

Minds are now free to fly.
Holding thought hand in hand,
In the hearts of none-to-believe,
At the end of sea and sand.

And finally...

Elliott Stein

I stand firmly and feel
the ground beneath, my
lovers hand in mine fasted.

For many years and a day,
I open my heart.

All the shades of poem
emerge for that special her.

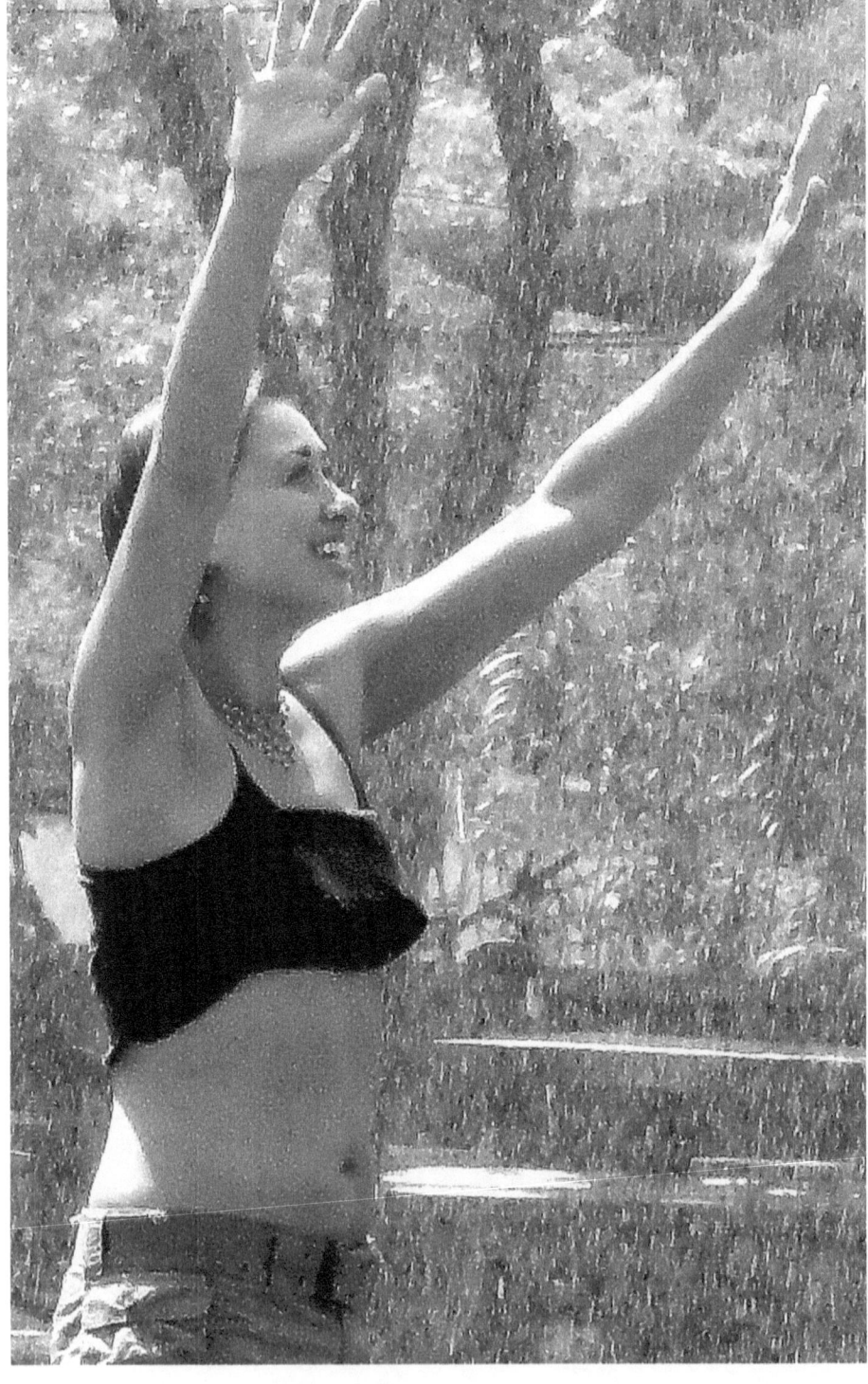

With You

I love you because…
I say so.
I speak it so real,
Reality flows from my heart,
Through endless time,
With you.

You are my soul mate because…
I believe it.
I feel it with my being,
The illusionary past lives to the future,
Across all incarnations,
With you.

Through our dreams you're part of me because…
I feel you.
We are always together,
Our connection is every moment,
It sings eternal,
With you.

Epilogue.

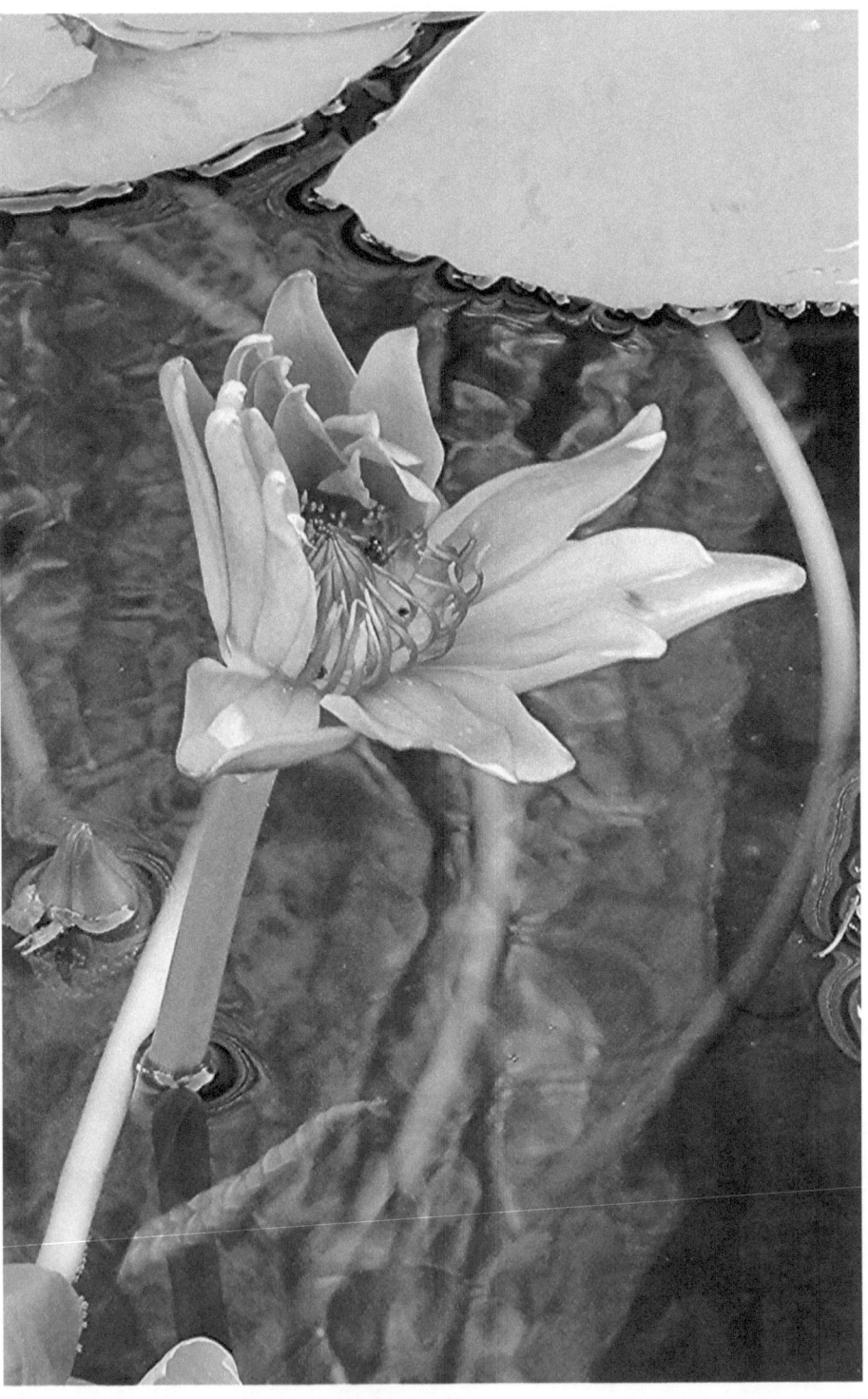

Thank you

I wrote this,
To gift you a piece of my soul.
I wanted to share my 'being',
With you.

I wrote this,
So we could have an intimate moment together.
I wanted to express my love,
To rant my torments and deepest fears.

I wrote this so we could laugh together,
I wanted to be plain silly and stupid with you.
I also wanted to make you feel sad and cry,
I wanted to penetrate deep into your heart.

I wanted to play with your mind,
To make you think and be in wonder.
To provoke you, tease you, shock you,
To move you, touch you, inspire you.

I wrote this,
To thank you,
For your generosity,
In reading this.
But mainly,
To just be with you.

www.ingramcontent.com/pod-product-compliance
Lightning Source LLC
Chambersburg PA
CBHW030918180526
45163CB00002B/386